Enterprise Mac
Managed Preferences

Edward Marczak and Greg Neagle

Apress®

Enterprise Mac Managed Preferences

ISBN-13 (pbk): 978-1-4302-2937-7

ISBN-13 (electronic): 978-1-4302-2938-4

Printed and bound in the United States of America 9 8 7 6 5 4 3 2 1

President and Publisher: Paul Manning
Lead Editor: Clay Andres
Technical Reviewer: Nigel Kersten
Editorial Board: Clay Andres, Steve Anglin, Mark Beckner, Ewan Buckingham, Gary Cornell, Jonathan Gennick, Jonathan Hassell, Michelle Lowman, Matthew Moodie, Duncan Parkes, Jeffrey Pepper, Frank Pohlmann, Douglas Pundick, Ben Renow-Clarke, Dominic Shakeshaft, Matt Wade, Tom Welsh
Coordinating Editor: Anita Castro
Copy Editor: Mary Ann Fugate
Production Support: Patrick Cunningham
Indexer: Potomac Indexers, LLC
Artist: April Milne
Cover Designer: Anna Ishchenko

Distributed to the book trade worldwide by Springer Science+Business Media, LLC., 233 Spring Street, 6th Floor, New York, NY 10013. Phone 1-800-SPRINGER, fax (201) 348-4505, e-mail orders-ny@springer-sbm.com, or visit www.springeronline.com.

For information on translations, please e-mail rights@apress.com, or visit www.apress.com.

Apress and friends of ED books may be purchased in bulk for academic, corporate, or promotional use. eBook versions and licenses are also available for most titles. For more information, reference our Special Bulk Sales–eBook Licensing web page at www.apress.com/info/bulksales.

The source code for this book is available to readers at www.apress.com. You will need to answer questions pertaining to this book in order to successfully download the code.

Contents at a Glance

Contents

About the Authors

Ed Marczak is a frequent speaker at technology conferences and the co-founder of MacTech Conference. He writes a monthly column for, and is the Executive Editor of MacTech Magazine. His days are currently spent on the Mac team at Google. Past the technology, Ed is a husband and father and enjoys travelling and playing music.

Greg Neagle is currently a senior systems engineer at a large animation studio. He has presented on Mac OS X management topics several times at the Macworld San Francisco and Apple's World Wide Developer Conferences, and is a columnist for MacTech magazine. Greg has been working with the Mac since 1984, and with OS X since its release. Greg also enjoys backpacking in the Grand Canyon and holds a black belt in taekwondo.

About the Technical Reviewer

Nigel Kersten is currently a Systems Administrator, specializing in Configuration Management at Google™.

Acknowledgments

While there are too many people for me to acknowledge, there are people that rise so high on my landscape that they can't escape my thanks. First thanks goes to my wife, Dorothy, and all of my family for always supporting my endeavors, even if it means seeing me a bit less while I'm sequestered away while writing and working. Immediately following that, I need to thank my co-author Greg Neagle. Choosing a partner for any project is often a make or break decision. I clearly chose the right person.

Technology is compelling, but only to a point. There are people that keep me interested beyond the technology. On that front, a big 'thank you' to Clay Caviness, Nigel Kersten and Dave Dribin.

There are people that inspire and lend their help when they are simply not required to. For that, I am very grateful to Neil Ticktin, Schoun Regan and Jussi-Pekka Mantere.

I wouldn't be where I am at all without teachers. There are people that have mentored me directly or indirectly, and have made me a better person in one way or another: Joseph Dries, Jonathan "Wolf" Rentzsch and Dr. Robert Marose, thank you.

Finally, thanks to everyone at Apress who believed in this topic and made this book a reality.

I'm sure I've forgotten some people that belong on this list. However, because I only know wonderful people, I'm sure they'll forgive the omission.

Edward Marczak

First, thanks to my co-author, Edward Marczak, for inviting me to join him in writing this book.

Thanks to members of the MacEnterprise group. Through mailing list and face-to-face discussions, I learned so much about Macintosh management techniques, Unix scripting, and more.

Thanks also to Nigel Kirsten, our technical reviewer for this book. Besides providing invaluable input on the this book's technical content, he's been a source of help, ideas and advice for as long as I've known him. It was during an informal discussion with Nigel and a few others that the original ideas for Local MCX were born.

Finally, I'd like to thank my wife, Allison, and my kids, Wyatt, Cassie, and Emma for putting up with me while I spent even more time than usual on the computer while working on this book.

Greg Neagle

Preface

Our goal in writing this book is to have a single definitive guide to Apple's Managed Preferences. We speak at conferences, participate on mailing lists, write blogs and magazine columns and work in Mac-heavy environments. We see Mac administrators on a daily basis asking questions about this facet of the operating system. The number one misconception about Apple's Managed Preferences is that in order to use it, you must have an OS X Server. This is not the case! You can take advantage of Managed Preferences no matter your environment: from one stand-alone Macintosh, to a handful of Macs in a Windows environment, to thousands of Macs surrounded by Unix servers. All it takes is a little knowledge, and a little elbow grease.

Owing to the phrase, "Give a man a fish and he will eat for a day. Teach a man to fish and he will eat for a lifetime," we want to *both* teach you to fish *and* give you a fish. We teach you the inner workings of Managed Preferences and everything it relies on. We also want to get you up and running quickly, so, there is also a chapter with Managed Preference recipies: step-by-step instructions that help you tackle the most common management issues straight away.

We've written this book using Mac OS X version 10.6, "Snow Leopard" as a guide, but all of the information is applicable to version 10.5, also. Much of it likely applies to 10.4, too, but we didn't test on that revision, as Apple no longer supports Mac OS X v10.4.

If you're a Windows administrator that just had a bunch of Macs thrust into your environment and are now responsible for dealing with them, this book is for you. While it's not quite Group Policy, Macs *are* manageable.

Many of you may already use an off the shelf system to manage Macintosh machines. Is this book for you? Yes, of course! Managed Preferences allow you to work in conjunction with your existing management system.

We've absolutely tried to wring out every facet of Managed Preferences that you must know about. This makes you a more complete Mac administrator and, in turn, makes your job easier. When you have your delivery infrastructure set up, being able to quickly deploy preferences when needed can make you a technological super hero. Enjoy your newfound powers!

Ed and Greg

## Chapter 1

Why Manage?

A personal computer is a wonderful thing. Not only do you have the tools available to perform your tasks, but you are also largely able to customize the tools and the computer environment itself. This is ideal when it's your one single *personal* computer. When that computer belongs to a fleet of machines—10, 50, 1,000, or more—variances among them may prove problematic. This is where client management comes in.

Client management, however, does not necessarily mean that every setting is locked down and the person who is ultimately using the machine can't change a thing (although it may). It may be set up as a convenience—to prepare a machine in a manner that people expect, even though it may be just freshly unboxed.

This book is about managing Macintosh OS X machines, focusing on Leopard and Snow Leopard. If you're a long-time Macintosh administrator in a completely OS X environment, we hope we have something a little deeper to share. If you're a longtime Macintosh administrator, but now find yourself in an environment without a Mac OS X server to manage the machines in your fleet, we can show you how—no matter if this is because you're in an all Windows environment, or if you don't have any formal server at all. Finally, if you're a Windows admin suddenly finding more and more Macintosh machines under your purview, never fear! Macintosh machines *are* manageable.

Mac OS X supports *Managed Preferences*, also called "MCX" by many administrators (this is because the directory record that stores the information are named "MCXSettings" and "MCXFlags," which purportedly stands for "Managed Client for (OS) X"). The Managed Preferences system is very powerful and extensible. However, it's somewhat under-documented and—we find—misunderstood. Managed Preferences is akin to Windows' Group Policy. It's similar in concept, but different in execution. In this chapter, we'll look at specific reasons for client management and take a high-level look at what's involved:

- The benefits you gain by managing machines

- The need to deliver these preferences to client machines

- Alternate ways to manage client machines outside of Managed Preferences proper

Predictability Means Less Work over Time

One great reason to manage is offering predictability to the people who will be using their machines. In a smaller company, people may not change machines too often, but correspondingly, the tech support staff will likely be smaller in number and might not want to manually set up each machine every time it is handed to someone. In a larger organization, the scale just becomes impossible to handle. Client management allows a machine to set certain default values for users so it's ready (or nearly ready) for use without much manual work.

For example, if there is an application that is used company-wide, it is convenient to have an icon for it in the Dock. Rather than rely on the end-users to add the icon, wouldn't it be nice if it could just appear there for them with no additional work on their part? This is just one way client management turns out to make computer use easier for both the end-user *and* the administrators.

Predictability also ties into your organization's default settings. If your company has decided to use Microsoft Word 2008, but keep the older non-XML formats for compatibility, you can set that automatically for all users. It's better to have it set from the start than to require people to remember to update the setting (and possibly having a few documents saved in the wrong format).

Maintaining Company Policy

Another reason to manage a machine is to align it with the policies of the company. Often, the policies enforced are security-related. This may mean automatically enabling FileVault on accounts as they are created, and disallowing the user to turn it off. It may mean enforcing a proxy for web traffic to pass though. There won't be a lecture here about how or why to have or follow a company policy, just to say that you can.

Sometimes, security policies are in place because they're solving a direct problem. In the example of enforcing FileVault for accounts, laptops are lost or stolen every day. It's useful to know that to the new person possessing the machine, it's just a shell, rather than a vessel to company data. Enforcing a password-protected screensaver is further protection for machines that are left logged-in and merely put to sleep by closing the lid. At other times, certain security policies exist to protect less tech-heavy users. For example, salespeople often travel outside of the office; they visit client sites, and work in hotel lobbies, conference rooms, and coffee shops, all of which are typical locations to use a laptop. They're also locations where one may step away from a laptop to refill a beverage or throw away trash, or get distracted by a conversation. A managed machine could be set to require a password for unlocking the screen saver and after waking from sleep, protecting the machine from passers-by who may want to sneak a peek at the screen or use it for unknown purposes while the owner is away.

Removing Unused Functions

Sometimes, people can find themselves lost in a sea of menu choices, check boxes, and other user-interface elements that they will simply never use for one reason or another. Sometimes these choices are against company policy. At other times, they lead the user down the wrong path.

Mac OS X's Managed Preferences system can often solve this. When a preference is set to never allow change, that option is typically then either grayed-out in the GUI, or hidden altogether. Alternatively, there may be an option that just gets in the way.

You may have a policy that all Apple software updates need to be tested before anyone in the company installs them. You may also have a way of forcing clients to install certain updates. In either case, you'd prefer that people don't install these updates. Apple doesn't help you here: a dialog box will pop up in front of the user, letting him or her know that there are updates waiting. Managed Preferences will let you disable this update check from ever occurring, if that's your approach.

Another example is one that we've had people ask us about repeatedly: "How can I turn off the 'Shared' computers in the sidebar?!?" For many people, seeing this list is annoying, and worse, possibly confusing. In a large organization, this list can grow too large to be useful—it simply wasn't designed to scale to large environments. As an administrator, Managed Preferences will help you eliminate this detritus if you so deem it.

Keeping Your Sanity

As a systems administrator, you face a huge number of challenges on a daily basis. Wouldn't you rather be looking at the big picture than handing the minutia of every machine on an individual basis? The idea with client management is that you have a central location to specify policy for groups of machines, or your entire fleet. Once specified, the policy applies itself, with no further work from you, the administrator. How it does this, as we'll find out, is a little situation-dependent. Once configured, though, policy should simply flow from the central location to client machines as they "check-in" with the management node.

Let's imagine that your company implements a new "green energy" policy that requires all desktop machines to enter sleep mode after being idle for 15 minutes. If you have 200 desktop machines across the company, possibly in different physical locations, how can you accomplish this?

You could walk to each machine yourself, of course. However, you may approach a machine only to find that it's busy and the owner asks you to come back another time. You're not going to meet any deadlines this way.

You could send out an e-mail to everyone in the company, asking them to open up the Energy Saver preference pane and make the adjustments themselves. However, you have no real guarantee that people will actually abide by this.

You could write a script that used SSH to connect to each machine, or use Apple Remote Desktop's "Send UNIX command" feature to send out a UNIX command to set the Energy Saver preferences. But that wouldn't reach machines that were off or asleep, or laptops that were out of the office. You'd need to keep checking for machines that didn't have this set and send the commands again.

With any of these strategies, you'd still have to remember to configure any new machines you purchased and deployed as well.

With a way to manage this centrally, though, you're in luck: you can apply the preference once, in one location, and have each machine under management respect your wishes. New machines would get the management settings as well. Isn't that a relief?

Another way that Managed Preferences can help your sanity as an administrator goes back to predictability: the machine should be predictable for you, too. When tech personnel need to alter settings manually for each machine they set up, often, certain settings are mistakenly skipped. Automating this allows the preference to be set properly once—in one central location—and it won't be forgotten. This cuts down on repeat visits after machine deployment.

Preference Delivery

The good news is that the Managed Preferences system for OS X is relatively easy to understand and implement. It's largely misunderstood by system administrators, due to a lack of exposure and convenient, thorough documentation. One thing you *do* need is a way to deliver these preferences to your fleet. Chapter 6, "Delivering Managed Preferences" is dedicated to just this topic and will dive into it more deeply.

If you're using OS X end-to-end (OS X Server and OS X clients), you bind your clients to Open Directory, set preferences using Apple tools, and it all just works. However, we're finding that there are more and more companies adding Macintosh computers to their fleet with no other Mac OS X infrastructure at all. Moving away from the pure Apple tool-chain can be a little confounding. While we'll cover the all-Apple scenario—which can be extended even past what Apple supplies you with—through this book, we're really focusing on the lone Mac in a Windows or Unix world variety.

The point is that preferences don't just magically appear on a client machine. You'll need *some* kind of infrastructure for delivery. That infrastructure may take the form of a directory service that clients can bind to, such as Open Directory or ActiveDirectory. It may even take the form of a script that runs periodically on a client (an "agent") that pulls preferences from a central location. Understand that this is a critical part of how you will deliver preferences.

Client Management Alternatives

This book is about managed preferences. You'll sometimes hear the phrase "client management" used interchangeably with "managed preferences." But "client management" can, and often does, refer to a wider range of management topics, like software installation, OS patch management, account creation and more.

There are many tools out there to help OS X administrators manage client machines. Some cover some aspects of client management; some cover other aspects. Some ship with OS X, some are available from Apple, some are open-source, and some are commercial third-party tools.

Scripting

Experienced UNIX administrators are often tempted to just write a bunch of scripts to help manage machines, and scripts can be used to manage preferences and settings.

Using scripts to manage OS X client machines is very powerful, but also presents many challenges. If you choose to write a script to configure or manage a certain setting in OS X, here are some of the problems you'll need to solve:

- Figuring out where the setting is stored; which file or datastore contains the settings you are interested in.

- Choosing the right tools to modify the setting. Do you need to use `defaults`, `PlistBuddy`, `systemsetup`, `networksetup`, `dscl`, or some combination of tools?

- Choosing a scripting language: OS X gives you an embarrassment of riches here. You have several different variations of shell languages (sh, csh, tsch, bash, and zsh), Perl, Python, Ruby, PHP, and even the old Mac stand-by, AppleScript, at your disposal. Some languages are better fits for certain tasks than others.

- Writing, testing, and debugging the script itself.

- Delivering the script to each machine.

- Getting the script to run in the appropriate context (e.g., as root, or as the current GUI user).

- Getting the script to run at the appropriate time (e.g., at startup, at login, or on a repeating basis).

For these last points, there are several Apple-supported ways to run scripts at specific times. Here are some:

- *StartupItems:* Available since OS X version 10.0, StartupItems are now deprecated, but still available for use. While we don't recommend using StartupItems for much of anything these days, you may find them around as a holdover from days gone by. Unfortunately, StartupItems are installed too often by commercial vendors who haven't learned the newer way of handling this under OS X. StartupItems run at boot time, before any user logs into the system.

- *Login Hooks:* When login hooks became available in OS X, many administrators rejoiced. A single script can be set to run when a user logs in. This script runs as root and is passed the ID of the user who is logging in (console logins only). This gives login hooks tremendous flexibility. Login hooks are a valuable part of OS X management. Huzzah!

- *Login items:* Most people are familiar with login items—programs set to run at user login. Users have control over adding to the list of items that run when they log in. This can be managed via the Dock, by choosing the "Open at Login" item from the contextual menu for a process on the Dock, or via the Accounts Preference Pane in System Preferences. Nicely, Apple's Managed Preferences can add to this list also.

- *Launchd Jobs:* Apple's launchd replaces the time-honored Unix cron daemon for job management. Actually, it replaces much more, with the ability to start jobs based on time (cron), to start jobs by listening to a socket (inetd), or to restart crashed jobs automatically (watchdog). Launchd is an excellent—and preferred—way to start jobs automatically at boot or based on the aforementioned criteria.

- *cron and periodic:* Even though launchd can replace the functionality of these traditional UNIX tools, if you are a seasoned UNIX administrator and comfortable with cron and periodic, they are still available and useful for running scripts on a repeating basis. However, cron and periodic have definite weaknesses when it comes to machines that may be off or asleep from time to time—if it's vital that a task run on a periodic basis, using launchd is a better choice.

This huge array of choices and options may be daunting, especially if you are new to managing OS X machines! Using Apple's Managed Preferences gives you a solid framework in which many of the previous challenges have been solved for you.

> **NOTE:** Using Apple's Managed Preferences tools may not free you entirely from the need to write scripts. In fact, in all likelihood, for a complete client management solution, you'll almost certainly need to use a combination of tools. Apple's Managed Preferences are just one more tool in your toolbox.

Managing Everything Else

Apple's Managed Preferences won't help you install software, or update the OS, or count the number of machines that have Photoshop installed, or manage software licensing. For those tasks, and others not mentioned here, you'll need to use other tools. We'll mention other tools at various places in this book, but here's a brief list of some of the more popular tools related to client management on OS X. These tools each have their own feature sets, but all cover some other elements of client management.

Apple Tools

- **Apple Remote Desktop**
  If you have no other management tool at your disposal, consider this one. A "jack-of-all-trades," it combines remote screen sharing with report generation, remote software installation, and more.

- **Apple Software Update Server**
  Part of OS X Server, this allows you to mirror Apple updates on a server inside your organization, saving the bandwidth costs of all your clients going out over the Internet to Apple's servers for updates. You can also choose to approve updates individually.

Open-Source Tools

- **Puppet**
  www.puppetlabs.com/
  Open-source systems configuration management

- **Radmind**
  http://rsug.itd.umich.edu/software/radmind/
  Filesystem management; used on OS X to install and remove software, and ensure the startup disk is always in a known state.

Third-Party Commercial Software

■ Casper Suite
www.jamfsoftware.com/

■ FileWave
www.filewave.com/

■ KACE Management Appliances
www.kace.com/

■ LANrev
www.lanrev.com/

This is not an exhaustive list. There are many more tools available, both open-source and commercial. All of these third-party packages do software installation and OS patch management. Some also support software inventory and license management. See each vendor's web site for more information.

A special mention for the Casper Suite: one of its many features is that it can provide a way to distribute managed preferences to client machines without needing an Open Directory server and without modifying an Active Directory or third-party LDAP service.

Summary

There are many reasons for wanting to manage a fleet of computers, and there are many ways to perform that management with Mac OS X. This chapter touched on just a few. While full management will likely require utilizing several methods at your disposal—Managed Preferences, scripting, and so on—Apple supplies the Managed Preferences system that is built right into Mac OS X, which is the focus of this book.

If you haven't yet looked into formal management of the machines in your purview, once you have, you'll wonder how you ever got along without it.

Chapter **2**

What Is the Managed Preferences System?

You're reading this book, so it's likely that you have some inkling of what the Managed Preferences system is. We've found that while many Mac administrators have a vague idea of what Managed Preferences are, they're looking for a deeper understanding of the system and some concrete examples of how to implement preferences that help them in their day-to-day tasks.

Apple's Managed Preferences in Mac OS X is a *policy framework*. As a framework, it doesn't really do anything on its own, but, rather, it lets you build what you require around it. Yes, this means a little work.

In this chapter, you'll learn how Managed Preferences came to be, what Managed Preferences actually are, what you can manage, and what you'll need to do so.

How Did We Get Here?

Pre-OS X Macintosh machines were, of course, revolutionary: a computer for "the rest of us." However, there was one thing they lacked in comparison to their DOS and Windows-running brethren—manageability. As computers populated businesses more and more, the ability to control the end-user experience helped DOS and Windows machines win the spot on business users' desks. Remember that the Macintosh had no lack of word processors, and Microsoft Excel showed up first on the Mac.

Typically, this manageability came in the form of DOS batch scripts that ran on machine startup, or at network login (the then-popular Novell NetWare allowed a central login script to run when a user successfully authenticated). Any Macintosh machines—usually located in an art department—were adrift and often required a dedicated admin. Naturally, businesses didn't like that too much.

> **NOTE:** Apple did make an early attempt at centralized management of Macintosh computers. The aptly named "Macintosh Manager" saw usage primarily in education environments. It was fairly expensive and Macintosh wasn't used heavily enough in most businesses for them to make the investment. By today's standards it would be considered crude, but it largely had the management features desired at the time. Managed Preferences are a bit of an outgrowth from this effort.
>
> Macintosh Manager managed only Mac OS 9 and the Classic environment. Apple supported this utility up through Mac OS X Server 10.3. It officially wouldn't run any longer under 10.4. While some lamented this decision, it's mostly because they liked to stick with what they knew. The contemporary technology is much better in terms of granularity and effectiveness than Macintosh Manager ever was.

Mac OS X, however, was built with the concepts of networking, multiple users, and permissions firmly in mind. Initially relying on a very traditional Unix model, Apple has now firmly put its own thumbprint on the methods that Mac OS X uses to support manageability in a modern setting.

The initial versions of Mac OS X understood the concepts, but not all of them were quite fully baked. That's enough history—fast-forward to today, when we're writing this book. Mac OS X v10.6, "Snow Leopard" is the current release. OS X *is* ten—happy birthday! Ten years is a good amount of time for a computer operating system to mature—and mature it has.

Apple's "thumbprint" on the course of Mac OS X has seen the transition from subsystems that were taken straight from BSD Unix to more modern, scalable subsystems. The new subsystems that Apple has put in place include the configuration daemon (configd), which is responsible for automatically configuring Mac OS X for its environment, the launch daemon (launchd), which is responsible for all manner of launching jobs and applications, and, of course, the Managed Preferences system (also called "MCX").

NOTE: When we talk about "modern systems," we're referring to being better suited to run on more contemporary architecture designs. Also, Unix has long been known to be scalable—but we need to stress that OS X is now designed to scale up *and* down. It's a single OS that runs on eight core MacPro machines with 8GB (or more) of RAM, down to a phone with an ARM processor and 256MB of RAM. How interesting is it that QuickTime X was originally written for the iPhone and then ported to full Mac OS X?

Where Are We Now?

Being the seventh version of a radical new operating system (Mac OS 9 it is *not*), Mac OS X v10.6 has solidified everything about the original Mac OS X v10.0 experience. Among these changes, the Managed Preferences system—introduced in Mac OS X 10.3—is Apple's solution to allow a centralized way of shaping the end-user's experience. As mentioned in Chapter 1, this may take the form of restrictions for security purposes. This may also take the form of creating a familiar environment that lets people hit the ground running when they use a new machine.

Since managed systems have existed for Windows for a longer period of time, it's easy to compare and contrast. Microsoft Windows uses *Group Policy* to manage Windows machines bound to Active Directory. These policy decisions are pushed down from the central Active Directory controller to Windows computers. Similarly, the easiest way to use Managed Preferences is to have Mac OS X Server running on your network. Once your computers are bound to this server running Apple's Open Directory, you can easily apply basic preferences to computers, groups of users, individual users, or in combination. This is often a reason that a Mac OS X Server is running on a network— the ease of client management.

Of course, the addition of a new server to a network may not be welcome. In many smaller shops, all-OS X may be the norm. In larger companies, though, there may already be a large investment in Unix or Windows servers that are not going to be removed for Mac OS X Server. Further, if Mac OS X clients are in the minority, it may be a burden on support staff to keep a Macintosh-based server up and running just for one purpose. (Of course, a smaller company may be in the same position, not wanting to invest in an additional server simply for client management.)

Fortunately, with a little additional work, but just as effectively, we can deliver managed preferences even without a Mac OS X Server. This will be demonstrated in later chapters.

The Heart of Managed Preferences

The very short answer to "what are managed preferences" is this: a managed preference is XML that is applied to a user, group, or computer record that alters the default behavior of the system or of an application. Managed preferences are stored in a directory service. This directory can be remote (Open Directory running on Mac OS X Server or ActiveDirectory on Windows Server, for example) or local (the local directory that's running on every Mac OS X 10.5 and 10.6 machine).

While the proper definition of managed preferences is the XML-in-a-directory just mentioned, we're going to extend it slightly. Mac OS X has a programmatic way to support preferences, called *User Defaults*.

A well-behaved OS X application uses the User Defaults methods to save and restore preferences. These preferences will be created in the user's own ~/Library/Preferences directory. It's essentially these preferences that are being managed with Managed Preferences ("MCX"). These preferences can be read outside of any application with either the GUI-based Property List Editor.app or the defaults command-line tool. These two utilities can read, alter, and write preference files, which are stored in the property list format.

As mentioned, Managed Preferences can be applied to an individual user (based on his or her credentials), to a group (based on group membership in a directory), to a computer (based on its UUID or MAC address (primary Ethernet)), or to a group of computers (based on membership in a directory). Since Mac OS X supports both network directory services and local directory services, you shouldn't be surprised to find that Managed Preferences don't need a network directory to function. You'll learn more about implementing Managed Preferences with different directory services in Chapter 6, "Delivering Managed Preferences."

When Managed Preferences are applied to a user, his or her session may behave differently than anyone else who logs into that particular machine. It will also be applied to the session no matter which directory-bound machine the user authenticates to via the GUI. Similarly, when Managed Preferences are applied to a group, all members of that group will have the same changes applied to their sessions no matter which directory-bound computer they log into. Finally, when Managed Preferences are applied to a computer or a computer that is a member of a managed computer group, anyone logging into that computer—without respect to user credentials or the groups that he or she belongs to—will have the same preferences applied. While this may sound a little complicated, it's pretty straightforward in practice. In each chapter, we'll cover a bit more about how these preferences are applied, how they interact with each other and, ultimately, how to debug them when they're not behaving as you'd expect. There's also an entire chapter dedicated to practical examples to guide you in creating your own preferences.

What Can You Manage?

You may be thinking, "Great! There's a management system built into OS X. But what exactly can it manage?"

The short answer is that Apple's Managed Preferences can help you manage almost anything that stores its settings in an Apple property list (".plist") file in the user's Library/Preferences directory.

More specifically, Managed Preferences can help you manage the following (not a complete list):

- System-wide settings
    - Energy Saver
    - Network
    - Bluetooth
    - Time Machine
    - Software Update server
    - Mobility settings (Portable Home Directories)
- Security
    - Login window
    - FileVault
    - Screen saver
    - Wake-from-sleep password
    - Secure VM
- User experience
    - Available applications
    - Available preference panes
    - Available printers
    - Use of removable disks
    - Desktop, Finder, Dashboard, and Dock
    - Automatic user account setup for Mail, iCal, and iChat
    - Web proxies

- Application settings
  - Save formats
  - Available features
  - Parental controls
  - Registration info
  - Suppress application updates

When it comes to individual applications, what you can manage varies greatly. Some Apple applications have lots of settings you can manage via managed preferences—others, not so many. Third-party applications can sometimes be managed as well. If the application stores a preference in a `.plist` file in the user's `Library/Preferences` folder, you will be able to manage that preference at some level.

What You Will Need

Everything you need to work with managed preferences is built into OS X. Other useful resources are available, but fortunately, they all come at little to no monetary cost. You should consider downloading and installing the following tools; they will be helpful when reviewing upcoming chapters:

- *Server Admin Tools*: This free download from Apple comes with several applications, but you'll need only one from the bundle—Workgroup Manager. As of this writing, the current Server Admin Tools package is version 10.6.3 and available from `http://support.apple.com/kb/DL1032`. Other versions are available from Apple's support section of their web site (`http://support.apple.com`). You may need an older version—for example, if you are still running Mac OS X v10.5.

- *Apple's Developer Tools*: This large download isn't *strictly* necessary. Like the Server Admin Tools package, there's only one thing you'll need from here—Property List Editor.app. (Technically, you can get by without that as well!) Apple provides the developer tools free of charge. You can either install them from the Mac OS X DVD that came with your computer, or download the most recent version from Apple's developer web site (`http://developer.apple.com`).

- *Your favorite programmer's editor*: You likely call this a "text editor," however, certain editors—like Text Edit.app or Microsoft Word—either don't save in plain text or use auto-correct to your disadvantage. You want a text editor that's on your side and makes your job easier. This could be vim (Ed's preferred editor, built into OS X and free), or a commercial product like TextMate (Greg's favorite), or BBEdit. Ideally, you'll have a good reason for choosing your editor.

You will also need the following:

- *Some scripting skills:* We're not asking you to become the next Donald Knuth. However, as a system administrator, you will always be better served by learning even the most basic scripting. Depending on how you plan to deliver managed preferences to your clients, some scripting may be involved. We'll present some sample scripts, and do our best to explain what is going on in them, but we can't cover shell scripting in depth in this book.

- *The desire to learn:* I know this one sounds trite, but like anything, the amount you get out of any book or lesson depends on *you*. We've been somewhat surprised at how little managed preferences are used or understood by many Macintosh administrators. If you're willing, though, you'll find it isn't difficult at all, and it can make your job as a system administrator much easier.

Nicely, these are all available at no cost. (Of course, BBEdit and TextMate are commercial products, but you can find similar functionality in products that are free, such as MacVim and TextWrangler.)

Summary

The Managed Preferences system ("MCX") has evolved over a period of time. It also continues to evolve, and what we see now is only the current manifestation. Everything that you need to work with MCX is either built into OS X or freely available. Of course, you can choose to use products that you purchase. You will be repaid for your study, tenacity, and experimentation with all of the facets of Managed Preferences, making your job as a system administrator easier.

## Chapter 3

Understanding Directory Services

In Mac OS X, managed preferences and directory services are intertwined. Managed preferences data is stored in directory services. Mac OS X machines use directory services to obtain information about users, groups, computers, services, and more. In this chapter, we'll discuss directory services, some common directory service configurations, and how directory services relate to managed preferences.

What Are Directory Services?

The term "directory service" refers to a store of information used by the operating system. Typically, this information store contains information about users and groups. It often contains information about computers and resources like printers and services, and may contain information about any entity that an administrator deems necessary. If this all sounds like a database, it effectively is. The difference is that a directory service refers only to the *interface* that allows access to this information without specifying the database or storage mechanism. Apple's Directory Service framework uses plug-ins that allow it to access many different data stores and other directory services. These include local flat files ("BSD"), local property list files, NIS, Microsoft's Active Directory, and LDAPv3.

The most common information stored in a directory service is user account information. As an example, for each user of a machine, the computer needs to keep track of items like the following:

- User name
- Password
- Location of the user's home directory

The computer needs to know the names of the users allowed to log in and their passwords, so it can verify that the person trying to log in is who he or she claims to be. Once a person has logged in, the computer needs to know where to find the user's data so it can make it available to the user.

In most cases, much more information is actually stored for each user, but this should get the basic idea across.

A directory service can, and usually does, keep track of information about things other than users. Information about user groups, computer objects, computer groups, network mounts, and service configurations is commonly stored in directory services.

Early in the history of computing, data like this was stored locally on each machine. This was a reasonable arrangement if there were a small number of "mainframe"-style computers that were accessed via dumb terminals. In an organization, if a user needed to be able to log in to multiple machines, the user account and other information needed to be created on each machine, or possibly copied from one master machine to all the others. If a user changed a password on one machine or for one server, the user would have to remember to log in to all of the other machines and servers and change the passwords there, or else keep track of multiple passwords. If the user were lucky, the organization's systems administrators might have implemented an automatic method of copying password files between machines.

But with the growth of computer networks and the personal computer revolution, organizations were quickly overwhelmed by the number of individual machines, each with its own local store of user account information.

This situation led to the development of centralized systems for storing this type of data. By storing the data in a central location that all the computers in an organization could access, the problem of keeping user information consistent across machines went away. With a consistent source of information about users and groups, access to shared resources became easier and more secure.

Central directory services granted additional advantages. With all the user account information stored in one place, it became possible to manage user access centrally. You could easily manage which computers and services a user had access to by making changes in the central directory. A user's password could be reset, or password complexity could be enforced. Employees leaving a company could have all computer access quickly removed.

But even today, small organizations may not use central directory services. If each machine typically has a single user, and there are few shared resources, account information may be local to each machine.

All Mac OS X machines have a local store of directory information, and they can be configured to use one or more centralized stores of directory information. If you are working in an organization that already has a central directory service, it's likely you can configure your OS X machines to use that service. If you don't currently have a central directory service, and you think your organization could benefit from one, Apple offers a network directory service as part of Mac OS X Server. It's probably not the best choice for a very large organization, but it is more than serviceable for workgroups and small to medium-sized organizations.

> **NOTE:** Setting up a central directory service is a huge topic. We cannot possibly do it justice within these pages. If you are interested in setting up Open Directory on Mac OS X Server, check out Apple's extensive documentation on the topic:
>
> http://images.apple.com/server/macosx/docs/Getting_Started_v10.6.pdf
>
> http://images.apple.com/server/macosx/docs/↵
> Open_Directory_Admin_v10.6.pdf
>
> http://images.apple.com/server/macosx/docs/User_Management_v10.6.pdf

Directory Services and Managed Preferences

Mac OS X's implementation of managed preferences relies on directory services. All of the data required to implement a managed preference policy is stored in a directory service.

If you have any experience with managing Microsoft Windows clients, this might sound familiar: Windows has a management system known as "Group Policy Objects" or "GPO," which is usually stored in Active Directory.

On Mac OS X, to manage preferences for a given user, group, computer, or group of computers, you'll need to store managed preferences data in a directory service. The directory service used for this is often a network directory service, but it can also be the local directory store. Since Mac OS X can communicate with multiple directory services at the same time, it's possible to store managed preferences in any available directory, not just the directory that contains your primary store of users and groups.

Directory Services Supported by Mac OS X

Mac OS X supports several different network directory services. It's no surprise that Apple's own Open Directory is supported, but it's also possible to use Mac OS X with several popular third-party directory services. Every Mac OS X machine also has a local directory service.

Open Directory

Open Directory is Apple's native centralized directory service. Hosted on Mac OS X Server, Open Directory is Apple's implementation of the LDAPv3 directory service and a secure password server, which allows OS X to store passwords in the various formats required by different network services in a secure fashion. Open Directory also includes a tightly integrated implementation of Kerberos 5, a popular system for providing a "single-sign-on" experience, where a user logs in once and is granted access to other Kerberos-aware services without having to log in for each service. Since Open Directory is part of Mac OS X Server, it supports Apple's Managed Preferences out of the box; no additional configuration is needed.

> **NOTE:** You'll see the term "Open Directory" used to mean two different things, which can lead to some confusion. Most commonly, "Open Directory" refers to Apple's network directory system hosted on Mac OS X Server, and based on OpenLDAP and MIT Kerberos. You may also see the term "Open Directory" used to refer to the flexible Directory Service framework available on Mac OS X, which uses plug-ins to communicate with various directory services (thus making it "open"). This flexible framework can be thought of as similar in concept to the NSS (Name Service Switch) modules available on other UNIX-like operating systems.

Active Directory

Active Directory is Microsoft's network directory service. It is probably the most commonly implemented network directory service, especially in the commercial world. Apple's support for Active Directory has steadily improved with each major release of Mac OS X. Active Directory does not natively support Apple's Managed Preferences, but it can be extended to do so. Later in this book, we'll show you how.

There are also third-party directory service plug-ins that replace or augment Apple's Active Directory support. These include Thursby ADmitMac, Likewise Enterprise, and Centrify DirectControl. You can use many of the techniques in this book with these alternate Active Directory plug-ins, but these plug-ins also provide additional options. For example, ADmitMac allows Active Directory administrators to use AD Group Policy to manage some things on Macs, and also allows Mac administrators to use Workgroup Manager and Apple's Managed Preferences. Likewise and Centrify's products are similar in this regard.

LDAPv3

LDAPv3 is a directory service protocol—that is, LDAPv3 describes a method for communicating with a directory service and a format for the results. LDAP stands for Lightweight Directory Access Protocol, so, technically, any directory service that can be accessed via the LDAP protocol can be called an LDAP server. There are many directory service implementations that are LDAPv3-compatible. Among them are Novell's eDirectory, OpenLDAP, and Red Hat Directory Server. In fact, Mac OS X uses the LDAPv3 protocol to communicate with Apple's own Open Directory. This shouldn't be surprising, since Apple's Open Directory is based on OpenLDAP. It is even possible to use the LDAPv3 protocol to work with Microsoft's Active Directory. You can store managed preferences data in any LDAPv3 directory by extending the schema. (A schema describes the records and attributes stored in the directory, so "extending the schema" refers to adding to the descriptions of records and attributes.)

NIS

NIS was one of the first popular centralized directory services. It was developed by Sun Microsystems and was very popular with organizations that had shared Solaris/UNIX/Linux infrastructures, especially those that used NFS as a shared file system. It has been largely replaced by the various LDAP implementations, but it is still supported in Mac OS X through Snow Leopard. It's not possible to use NIS as a source of managed preferences data, so if your organization uses NIS as its central directory store, you'll need to store managed preferences data in another directory. We'll discuss using multiple directories later in this chapter.

Local Directory Services

Every Mac OS X computer has a local directory service. This only makes sense, since not every Mac is used in a large organization. Since even Macs used at home have support for multiple users and access controls for various services, the OS needs a local place to keep track of such information. This is often referred to as "Local DS," which is short for "Local Directory Service." (You'll also see "DSLocal," which is another name for the same thing. In OS X 10.5 and later, the local directory service stores its data in */private/var/db/dslocal*, thus the name "DSLocal.")

Additionally, since laptops are not always on an organization's network, the local directory service takes on additional significance. A network directory service quickly loses its appeal on a laptop that's not connected to the organization's network. A laptop user who can't log in to his or her machine when at home isn't going to get much work done. On laptops, user accounts, at least, must be stored in the local directory service to allow access at all times. But this could bring us right back to the original problem of keeping the user account information consistent across an organization. If the user changes the password on his or her laptop, but doesn't remember (or know) to change it in the network directory as well, the user may be puzzled or annoyed (or worse) when he or she can't log in to his or her email account.

Mac OS X has a solution for this particular problem: mobile accounts. A mobile account is a user account whose information originates in a network directory service, but is cached in the local directory service. This provides the benefits of a network account, while still allowing access when the laptop is offline. Changes in the network account information are synchronized with the locally-cached account, and vice-versa. Mobile accounts retain their managed preferences when the machine is not connected to the enterprise network. Apple has also provided useful mobile account–specific preferences you can manage to help implement mobile accounts in your organization.

Directory Service Configurations

We've seen that Mac OS X supports multiple directory services. You can configure a Mac to talk to Open Directory or Active Directory, or rely only on a local directory service. But there's more—Mac OS X can utilize multiple directory services *at the same time*. Let's look at some possible configurations.

Local Only

The simplest configuration is the one every Mac has when you take it out of the box—a single directory service, the local directory. In fact, you cannot remove this directory service—Mac OS X always uses it. This is where information for all the local users is stored. These are the users you can see in the Accounts pane of System Preferences. There are also local users that do not appear in the Accounts pane. One example is "root," the most powerful user on OS X and other UNIX-like systems. There are many other hidden, special-purpose users and groups, and other information stored in the local directory service.

Network Directory Service

It's common to think that when you configure OS X to use a network directory service, such as Open Directory or Active Directory, this is the only directory service. But that's not the case—the local directory service is still there and still being used. In fact, OS X gives the local directory service higher priority than a network directory. This comes into play if there are directory records of the same name in multiple directory services. A user record for "jsmith" in the local directory service would take precedence over a user record for "jsmith" in a network directory service.

We can see a visual representation of the order of precedence in Directory Utility, Apple's tool for configuring OS X's connections to directory services. In Figure 3-1, you can see that "/Local/Default" and "/BSD/local" have a higher precedence than the Open Directory server "ldap.pretendco.com". (We'll ignore "/BSD/local" for now; it is not used by default in OS X and can usually be safely ignored.)

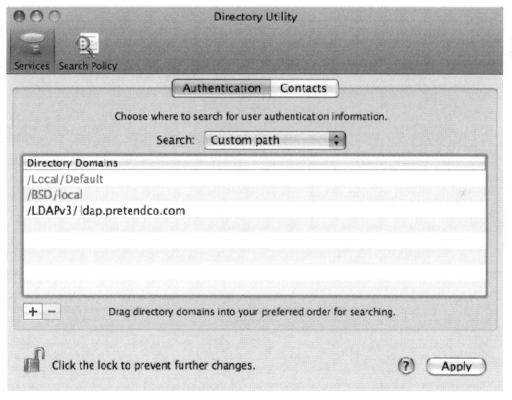

Figure 3-1. *Directory search path in Directory Utility*

NOTE: Are you still curious about **/BSD/local**, even though I said we can safely ignore it? This directory service node represents the traditional UNIX "flat file" storage of user, group, and other information. If your organization uses UNIX flat files on other platforms, you can configure Mac OS X to also use these files. Traditionally on most UNIX-like operating systems, these files live in */etc* and have names like the following:

/etc/master.passwd
/etc/group
/etc/hosts
/etc/networks
/etc/aliases
/etc/netgroup

The /BSD/local node is not normally used on Mac OS X. You can use Directory Utility to activate this node by configuring the "BSD Flat File and NIS" service. The /BSD/local node will then be searched after the /Local/Default node, but before any network directory services.

Remember that since **/Local/Default** has a higher precedence than **/BSD/local**, a root password (for example) in */etc/master.passwd* will not be consulted, since there is (normally) a record for root in /Local/Default.

Since managed preferences aren't a traditional UNIX service, it should come as no surprise that there's no way to store managed preferences data in the /BSD/local node.

See Apple's Open Directory documentation, `http://images.apple.com/server/macosx/docs/Open_Directory_Admin_v10.6.pdf`, if you'd like more info on the /BSD/local node.

You'll notice also that the local sources are grayed out—you cannot remove them, nor can you change their order. The order in which directory services are searched for information is called the "search path." If user "John Smith" tried to log in to this Mac, first the local directory would be searched for information on John. If no information for John Smith was found in the local directory service, then the Open Directory server "ldap.pretendco.com" would be queried for information about John.

What happens if more than one directory service has information about John Smith? The first one in the search path "wins." That is to say, if there are user accounts for John Smith in both /Local/Default and in the LDAPv3 directory, when John Smith tries to log in, he'd better use the password stored in the local directory. If he uses the password for his network account, it will fail to authenticate him, as OS X will never consult the LDAPv3 directory for his account information, since it found account information for him in the local directory. Assuming he uses the password from the local directory, he'll be authenticated and get the home directory that is also defined in the local directory. It is as if the account information in the LDAPv3 directory doesn't even exist.

A special case of an account that exists in both a local and network directory is a mobile account, as discussed earlier in this chapter. In this case, the account information is kept synchronized between the two directory services, allowing a laptop user to use his or her network credentials, even when not connected to the company's network. A mobile account can be thought of as a network account that is cached in the local directory service. It retains an attribute that allows the OS to find the original record in the network directory service when needed and available.

Multiple Network Directory Services

Even when you are using a single *network* directory, Mac OS X is consulting multiple directories. As we've seen, Mac OS X searches the /Local/Default node in addition to a network directory. You can take this concept one step further and configure multiple network directory services.

One common configuration is sometimes known as the "Magic Triangle" or "Dual Directory" (Figure 3-2). This is one solution to the problem of not being able to add Mac-specific data to a central directory service. In the magic triangle, a Mac is configured to use two network directory services. Often one service is Active Directory, and the second is Open Directory. This allows the Mac to get company-wide user and group information from the enterprise directory service (Active Directory), and to get Mac-specific information from Open Directory on Mac OS X.

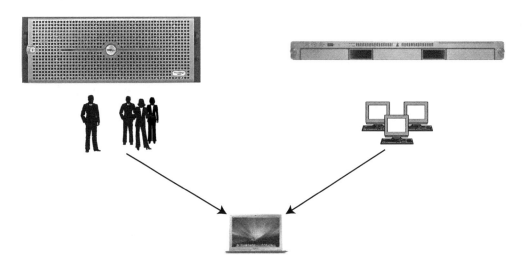

Figure 3-2. *The "Magic Triangle"*

The two directories need not be Active Directory and Open Directory; you might set up a magic triangle where both directories were LDAPv3 directories. One LDAPv3 directory service might be a large education site's central directory, and the other LDAPv3 directory might be a small department's directory server running on a Fedora box.

Starting with Mac OS X 10.5 "Leopard," Apple extended the ideas behind the Magic Triangle or Dual Directory by introducing "augmented records." Augmented records allow a Mac OS X administrator to "virtually" add additional attributes to a record in an existing directory service by creating a related record in a secondary directory service. For example, this allows you to add Mac-specific attributes to user records coming from a central network directory service without having to modify the records in the central service. Mac OS X virtually merges the data coming from both directory services to make a single virtual record containing all the attributes from both directories. You could use augmented records on an Open Directory server to store managed preferences data for a user account stored in an Active Directory domain.

Later in this book, we'll also look at another variation on the idea of supplementing a central directory by storing managed preferences data in another directory. Specifically, we'll describe using a local directory data store for managed preferences data in conjunction with Active Directory or a third-party LDAPv3 directory.

Summary

In this chapter we've presented a quick introduction to directory services. We discussed the various directory services supported by Mac OS X and talked about common directory service configurations. We also noted how directory services and managed preferences are connected—on Mac OS X, managed preferences are stored in a directory service. We'll get into the details of this in Chapter 5, "Delivering Managed Preferences."

Chapter **4**

Property List Files

The property list file format (`.plist`) is at the heart of many operations in Mac OS X. As a well-structured XML document, the `.plist` format is easy to parse programmatically. The format is important to understand, as Apple's preferences are currently stored in `.plist` files (however, Apple makes no guarantees of this format going forward). Not coincidentally, Managed Preferences are stored and delivered in a formatted `.plist` file, too. There are several tools available on Mac OS X that allow you to work with `.plist` files. These include Property List Editor.app and the `plutil`, `defaults`, and `PlistBuddy` command-line tools. Because `.plist` is the native format for Managed Preferences, it's essential for an administrator to understand the contents of a `.plist` file, and how to work with them.

Therefore, we start this chapter with an overview of the `.plist` format, followed by an actual example that shows how Managed Preferences are stored and delivered in a `.plist` file. We then walk through the aforementioned tools that will help you deal with the `.plist` format.

What Are Property List Files?

Simply put, property list files are well-formed ("structured") XML files that store keys and values. Keys are like labels or variable names. `.plist` files store simple hierarchies of data. The types of data that can be stored in a `.plist` file are ostensibly limited to a few chosen types, but one type—binary data—can effectively store any binary value. The basic types that a `.plist` file can store are strings, numbers, binary data, dates, and Boolean values. There are also container types. A container isn't any type itself, but contains basic types or other containers. The container types are arrays and dictionaries.

> **NOTE:** These types weren't chosen arbitrarily: each type in a property list file has a corresponding class in Apple's programming frameworks, specifically the NSDictionary class. The NSDictionary class has methods that read and write .plist files (Table 4-1).

Table 4-1. *Valid XML Types for a Property List*

XML/Plist Type	Cocoa Class
<array>	NSArray – Container for other classes
<dict>	NSDictionary – Container for other classes.
<string>	NSString – Stores string data.
<data>	NSData – Stores arbitrary data. This data is base-64 encoded once written to the .plist file.
<date>	NSDate – For storing date values.
<integer>	NSNumber (intValue) – Class to store integer values.
<real>	NSNumber (floatValue) – Class for floating point values.
<true/> or <false/>	NSNumber (boolValue == YES or boolValue == NO) – The <true/ > and <false /> elements are interpreted as Boolean values.

> **NOTE:** NSDictionary is the perfect partner for .plist files. If you need to access .plist files programmatically, make your best effort to use a language that can use Cocoa—namely, Objective-C, Python, or Ruby. To get the contents of a .plist file into an NSDictionary, use the dictionaryWithContentsOfFile: or dictionaryWithContentsOfURL: methods. To write an NSDictionary as a .plist file, use the writeToFile:atomically: method. See the "Resources" section at the end of this chapter for links to further documentation.

In Apple's Cocoa framework, the corresponding classes are NSString, NSDate, NSData, NSNumber, NSArray, and NSDictionary itself. These classes map directly to the value-types in a .plist file. In short, it's no mistake that Mac OS X developers store data in .plist files. There happens to be one other reason, too.

Mac OS X developers have another useful routine in their toolbox: the user defaults system. Anytime a well-behaved Mac OS X program wants to save its preferences, it uses the user defaults system. As it turns out, the user defaults system is optimized for—and will work only with—values that can be stored in .plist files. (See where we're going with this?)

These preferences are stored in well-defined places:

- Preferences for just one user are stored in that user's home directory in Library/Preferences. An example of this would be iTunes preferences. Each person on a single system will have a different iTunes setup: window position, artwork hidden or displayed, and so on. This is stored as ~/Library/Preferences/com.apple.iTunes.plist.

- Inside the user's Library/Preferences folder is another folder named ByHost. Inside it are per-user preferences that apply only to a specific machine. The intent of these "ByHost" preferences is for users who have network or portable home directories, and who also use multiple machines, to be able to have unique preferences for each machine they use. An example is the com.apple.preference.displays set of preferences (or *preference domain*)—if you had a network home directory, and sometimes logged into a machine that had two 19-inch displays connected to it, and sometimes logged into a machine that had a single 30-inch display connected, it's far more useful to be able to keep your display preferences separate for each machine. These "ByHost" preferences are named in the format com.apple.preference.displays.XXXXXXXXX.plist, where XXXXXXXXX is a unique identifier for each machine.

> **NOTE:** Apple has used two different methods to generate the unique machine identifier for ByHost preference names. The older style used the machine's Media Access Control (MAC) address. This was silently switched to use the machine's Universally Unique Identifier (UUID) to support the new MacBook Air which didn't have a built-in Ethernet port. Changing the AirPort card on these machines would also change the en0 MAC address, even if the motherboard was untouched.
>
> The current machine UUID is stored in the I/O Registry and can be retrieved using System Profiler, or the ioreg command:
>
> ```
> ioreg -rd1 -c IOPlatformExpertDevice | grep IOPlatformUUID
> ```
>
> This perhaps should make the point clear: the best method of managing these preferences is with Managed Preferences!

- Preferences for everyone on the machine are stored in /Library/Preferences (note the leading slash character, denoting that this Library folder is at the root of the drive). An example of a preference that is used system-wide is the Login Window. The way the Login Window is configured affects everyone on the system. Since it is typically displayed even before any single user logs in, its preferences *can't* be tied to any one user. Login Window preferences are stored as /Library/Preferences/com.apple.loginwindow.plist.

- Network-based preferences can be implemented by storing property lists in /Network/Library/Preferences. This works only for computers that are bound to a central directory service. It's not often used and has largely been supplanted by Managed Preferences. This location is merely mentioned for completeness.

You may notice that each of the example file names uses a similar naming scheme. This is called "reverse DNS naming." This helps identify where a preference file originated. Both the company URL and specific program name are part of the file name. It's not just Apple that follows this convention. For example, you may also find on your system com.microsoft.Word.plist, com.vmware.fusion.plist, and com.omnigroup.OmniFocus.plist.

> **NOTE:** The convention of using reverse DNS naming is just that—a convention. It is not enforced by the operating system on any level. Less informed developers have been known to shirk this unwritten rule and store their preferences in a file with a name that is obviously not like the others. Admin beware.

All of that said, .plist files are not restricted to the defaults system. Even Apple makes use of them outside of the paths listed previously for all sorts of data storage needs. For example, the bulk of the local directory is implemented via .plist files. (Take a peek in /var/db/dslocal/nodes/Default/Users—you'll need to be root to do so.) Another example is Apple's own launchd daemon. It is fed information about which jobs to run and when by .plist files. (Again, go peek in /System/Library/LaunchAgents and look at the types of files in there.)

Now that you've heard so much about property lists and their virtues, let's dive into the format itself.

Property List Example

Let's take a look at a very simple but realistic .plist file. This is plain text and can be (re)created in any text editor:

```
<?xml version="1.0" encoding="UTF-8"?>
<!DOCTYPE plist PUBLIC "-//Apple//DTD PLIST 1.0//EN"
"http://www.apple.com/DTDs/PropertyList-1.0.dtd">
<plist version="1.0">
<dict>
        <key>color</key>
        <string>blue</string>
        <key>count</key>
        <integer>15</integer>
        <key>style</key>
        <string>fruit</string>
</dict>
</plist>
```

If you're familiar with any markup, particularly HTML, this should all look a little familiar. The words contained in angle brackets are called "tags" and are part of the roadmap to the XML parser that is reading this file. Certain tags are "one-offs"—they appear and make a specification, but don't have a close. Other tags have an opening tag, enclose some value, and then must be explicitly closed. Closing tags match opening tags but start with a slash character after the opening angle bracket. In the example presented, this is illustrated by the "<key>...</key>" tags.

Indentation is a convention for human readability. In Apple .plist files, indents are formed by tabs, not spaces. In fact, some Apple utilities will tidy a .plist file on write to use tab indents where none existed before. While not strictly required, indenting according to hierarchy is good practice.

Now that we're on the same page terminology-wise, let's look more closely at the example presented.

Digging Deeper . . .

The header portion of the file declares this file as an XML file type:

```
<?xml version="1.0" encoding="UTF-8"?>
<!DOCTYPE plist PUBLIC "-//Apple//DTD PLIST 1.0//EN"
"http://www.apple.com/DTDs/PropertyList-1.0.dtd">
```

Ultimately, this header isn't up to you. Apple's Cocoa APIs will properly generate and write this part of a property list. If you're creating a .plist file from scratch in a text editor, you should just copy this portion from another valid .plist file. For more information about XML, see the specification page at http://xml.org, or the Wikipedia entry at http://en.wikipedia.org/wiki/Xml.

> **NOTE:** Currently, different Apple utilities write the header with slight differences. Some launchd .plist files use the following:
>
> ```
> <!DOCTYPE plist PUBLIC "-//Apple Computer//DTD PLIST 1.0//EN"
> "http://www.apple.com/DTDs/PropertyList-1.0.dtd">
> ```
>
> NSDefaults writes .plist files with the following:
>
> ```
> <!DOCTYPE plist PUBLIC "-//Apple//DTD PLIST 1.0//EN"
> "http://www.apple.com/DTDs/PropertyList-1.0.dtd">
> ```
>
> While either header is perfectly valid and won't stop the .plist file from being used, it can trip you up if you're expecting a certain header. For instance, if you use Puppet or Radmind to manage your machines, take note that the same .plist information created with different Apple tools may cause your management system to detect a change and rewrite the file.

The .plist tag wraps the entire file:

```
<plist version="1.0">
```

Again, Apple's APIs will write this out as appropriate, and you should have this line in any .plist file that you create. Next, we find a dictionary tag:

```
<dict>
```

As mentioned earlier, one of the Cocoa classes that is easily transferrable to and from a .plist file is an NSDictionary, and that is what is shown here.

Wrapped in the dictionary are its *keys* and their corresponding *values*:

```
<key>color</key>
<string>blue</string>
<key>count</key>
<integer>15</integer>
<key>style</key>
<string>fruit</string>
```

This dictionary contains three keys: "color," "count," and "style." The "color" and "style" keys are string types, while "count" is an integer type. The *value* of the "count" key is "15".

Following this, the tags are closed and the file ends:

```
</dict>
</plist>
```

Each tag should lead to a new level of indentation, making it easy to see the hierarchical structure. Best of all, it's easily human-readable.

However, beginning with OS X 10.5, the bulk of .plist files found on the system are stored in a binary format, not plain text. While this does have the effect of using less space on disk and producing faster load times, it takes the human-readable part out of the picture. Of course, there are ways to deal with that, discussed in the following section.

> **NOTE:** You'll know a binary .plist file when you see one: it looks like gibberish as plain text. Apple's defaults command can properly read plain-text ("XML1") or binary .plist files. The defaults command will always *write* a .plist file as binary, however.
>
> If you're going to use the Cocoa NSDictionary class to read, manipulate, and write .plist files, you probably won't be surprised to find no problems here. Property lists written with writeToFile:atomically are written as XML1 (human-readable text) and files read with dictionaryWithContentsOfFile can be either XML1 or binary1.
>
> Note that if you're a Python or Ruby programmer, not all libraries support the binary .plist format.

As the use of property lists has evolved, the format has changed slightly. Property list files actually hearken back to the days of NeXT Computer and NeXTStep/OpenStep. Due to this, Apple supports three different variations of .plist files. The oldest of these is an ASCII-style .plist format inherited from NeXT. Its use is deprecated and we won't discuss it further. The two types you'll find present on a contemporary Mac OS X system are the XML representation and a binary format. The XML .plist format is represented in the example given previously. A purely visual display of a binary .plist format doesn't really make sense, so we won't show it here.

Each .plist format has advantages. XML-based .plist files are human-readable and easily portable. Binary .plist files are more compact and, therefore, use less memory and can be read and written more quickly. It's pretty clear why Apple has largely moved to the binary-based .plist format.

Working with Property List Files

Now that you know what property lists are supposed to look like, there must be some way to read and write them. Apple provides several ways to do so (Property List Editor.app and the plutil, defaults, and PlistBuddy command line tools), all of which are discussed in the next sections.

> **NOTE:** If you haven't installed the developer tools mentioned in Chapter 2, now is the time to do so. You'll need to install them to use Property List Editor, shown next, and in subsequent chapters throughout the book.

Property List Editor.app

One of the utilities that Apple provides to manipulate property list files is Property List Editor.app. Property List Editor can create, read, and write property lists. It's often the easiest way to visualize a .plist file. It's also useful for creating a .plist file from scratch, as Property List Editor.app will write the XML header and basic structure for you.

The Property List Editor application is installed as part of Apple's developer tools. Instructions for installing the developer tools are in Chapter 2. Once it is installed, you'll find it, along with a host of other tools, in the /Developer/Applications/Utilities folder (Figure 4-1).

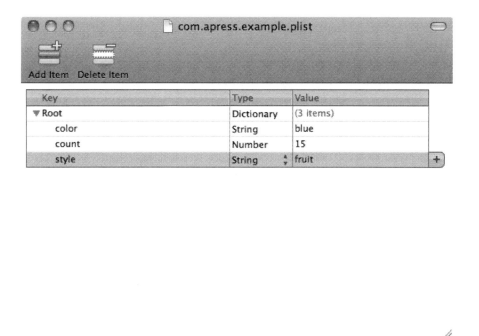

Figure 4-1. *Property List Editor.app displaying our example .plist file*

Using Property List Editor is very straightforward. If you read a .plist file, the structure and keys are displayed along the column on the left, and values are displayed in the column on the right. A center column lists the data type of the corresponding value in a given row. The two buttons in the top toolbar allow additions and deletions to the current .plist file. The delete button will remove an entire nested hierarchy, so be careful with it.

When saving a .plist file for the first time, or, by choosing Save As... from the File menu, you can choose a .plist format for the file (Figure 4-2). Property List Editor handles some very specific cases, and offers you five types of formats to save in. However, this book is concerned only with the first two offered: XML and binary.

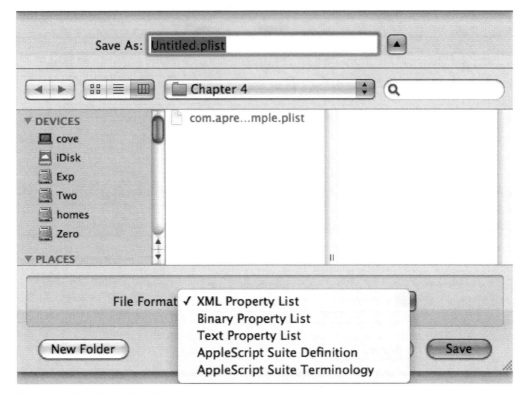

Figure 4-2. *Save dialog displaying the file format choices*

Creating a Property List from Scratch with Property List Editor

Property List Editor is useful for initially creating .plist files. Here's a quick overview:

1. Open Property List Editor.app from the /Developer/Applications/ Utilities folder on your local drive. (You've installed Apple's Developer Tools by now, haven't you? Without them, you won't have Property List Editor.app.)

2. By default, a new, untitled window is displayed. If you just want the framework for a .plist file with the proper headers, you can save this "empty" file with the Save... menu item in the File menu. See step 5 for more information about the Save dialog.

3. You can add keys and values with the Add Child button in the toolbar. Everything is a child of the root, so even an initial entry is a child with a parent entry to refer to.

4. Once you're done adding entries, save the file using the Save… menu item in the File menu.

5. Choose the type of .plist file you want to save, as shown in Figure 4-2. XML is human-readable text, useful if you're going to perform further editing or need a way to inspect the text without using Property List Editor.app. Binary is more efficient, but not human-readable, so is more appropriate for a .plist file in a final state.

It's a straightforward process; however, Property List Editor isn't easily automated. To automate manipulating .plist files, see the following section on command-line utilities.

Command-Line Utilities

Property List Editor is useful for getting your feet wet and very basic tasks. It has some shortcomings, though. Namely, the problem is scalability. If you need to manipulate a .plist file on more than one machine—let's say 500—Property List Editor would be a tedious way to manage. What if you need to update these .plist files from home, all automatically? This is what shell scripts and command-line utilities were designed for. There are three command-line tools that ship with Mac OS X: plutil, defaults, and PlistBuddy. Each has a different purpose and different capabilities.

plutil

plutil is the most basic and utilitarian of the three. plutil, the .plist utility, converts .plist files between text (XML) and binary formats and can also verify the structure of a .plist file. An example is in order. If you want to view the contents of a binary .plist file—com.apple.nat.plist, for example—but don't want to open it in Property List Editor, you can run the following:

```
plutil -convert xml1 -o - /Library/Preferences/com.apple.nat.plist
```

Running this command tells plutil to convert the .plist file to text ("xml1") and send the output ("-o") to standard out. If you wanted to store the file, you could write the output to a file on disk.

plutil can also "lint" a file—that is, check it for consistency and basic errors. What it cannot do is verify that your key-names and data are correct. Running a lint check is as simple as using the -lint switch:

```
$ plutil -lint /Library/Preferences/com.apple.loginwindow.plist
/Library/Preferences/com.apple.loginwindow.plist: OK
```

If the lint process encounters an error (or errors, perhaps), you're told the error and on which line:

```
$ plutil -lint someplist
someplist: Encountered unknown tag stringblue</string on line 6
```

defaults

The defaults command gives you access to the user defaults system. As mentioned, the "user defaults system" is a fancy way of saying "preferences," which, as you know by now, is just data stored in a .plist (for today: Apple reserves the right to change this format). The name is derived from the Cocoa API that performs the same task: NSUserDefaults. The defaults utility allows for reading and writing individual keys and their data to and from a .plist file, reading a .plist file in whole, and more.

Perhaps the simplest use of the defaults command is reading an entire .plist file. This is equivalent to the plutil command given earlier:

```
$ defaults read /Library/Preferences/com.apple.nat
{
    NatPortMapDisabled = 0;
}
```

You'll note that the output of the defaults command is concerned only with keys and their values. It does not output the XML header and closing tags.

The defaults command reads .plist files of either XML or binary. However, it will write a .plist file out only in the binary variety. It will even go so far as to convert an XML .plist file into binary if used to update a value in that .plist file.

As it's intdended to be used to manage "defaults" (Core Foundation Preferences) and not .plist files, the defaults command is very particular—when you ask it to operate on a specific .plist file, you must give it the absolute path and leave off the .plist extension. This is very unlike most command-line tools that operate on files, and it takes some getting used to. The fact that the defaults command operates on .plist files is a happy coincidence that we can take advantage of.

> **NOTE:** If you're using the `defaults` command in a script, you should be aware of certain behaviors (in addition to the leave-the-`.plist`-extension-off-of-the-file-name oddity). First, you shouldn't change the defaults of a running application. If you make a change to a running application, at best, the change won't be recognized. At worst, it may save on exit and wipe out your change or possibly corrupt the `.plist` file. Secondly, the `defaults` command does not have a wide range of exit codes: 0 for success and 1 for a failure of any type.

If you do not specify an absolute path, `defaults` looks for a preference domain for the current user. The following command will read the HomeSync preferences for the current user, *not* a file named `com.apple.homeSync` or `com.apple.homeSync.plist` in the current directory.

```
defaults read com.apple.homeSync
```

The `defaults` command, therefore, is not exactly a general-purpose `.plist` utility like `plutil` or Property List Editor.app. As mentioned, it works within the bounds of the user defaults system. The upshot of this is that it expects `.plist` files to reside in specific places: one of the `Library/Preferences` directories on the system. Apple does not recommend using the `defaults` command to read and write arbitrary `.plist` files. (While in 10.5 and 10.6, accessing arbitrary `.plist` files is possible, as part of the user defaults system, this functionality may go away.)

> **CAUTION:** The `defaults` command will be changed in an upcoming major release to operate only on preferences domains. General `.plist` manipulation utilities will be folded into a different command-line program.
>
> You have been warned! Fortunately, Apple does ship another general `.plist` manipulation command-line program, `PlistBuddy`, which we'll examine shortly.

To read one particular key from a `.plist` file, specify that key as an argument:

```
defaults read com.apple.finder WarnOnEmptyTrash
0
```

> **NOTE:** When requesting a specific key, the `defaults` command does not need to reprint that information and just gives the value.

To write a value to a .plist file, specify the key and the value, separated by spaces, as arguments on the command line:

```
defaults write com.apple.safari IncludeDebugMenu 1
```

It's good practice to include the data type of the value. For example, to ensure that a value is treated as an integer and not a string, use the -int specifier:

```
defaults write com.apple.safari includeDebugMenu -int 1
```

When no type is specified, the defaults command assumes a type of string. If you don't know the correct type for a given key, defaults can tell you:

```
defaults read-type com.apple.homeSync periodicSyncOn
Type is boolean
```

Since it's primarily designed to work with preference domains, and not actual files, the defaults command can also easily work with the ByHost preferences we mentioned earlier, without you having to figure out the specific file:

```
defaults -currentHost read com.apple.screensaver askForPassword
1
```

This can be more challenging with other tools, since you have to figure out the unique identifier for the current machine and use that to determine the correct file name to operate on.

One other small problem with defaults: it's clumsy to work with values in nested dictionaries.

PlistBuddy

PlistBuddy started off as a utility that was found embedded only in packages for Apple updates. Clearly, Apple realized they needed a utility like this and developed it for their own use. As of Leopard, though, it became a real part of the OS: it is found at /usr/libexec/PlistBuddy and even has a main page. While the defaults command can handle most tasks, PlistBuddy excels at editing keys and values in a nested dictionary.

> **NOTE:** The /usr/libexec path is not in the $PATH variable supplied by a default Mac OS X install. You'll always need to specify the full path to PlistBuddy in this case.

We need a slightly more complex example, so use the following .plist file, which contains a nested dictionary:

```
<?xml version="1.0" encoding="UTF-8"?>
<!DOCTYPE plist PUBLIC "-//Apple//DTD PLIST 1.0//EN"
"http://www.apple.com/DTDs/PropertyList-1.0.dtd">
<plist version="1.0">
<dict>
        <key>color</key>
        <string>blue</string>
        <key>count</key>
        <integer>15</integer>
        <key>cust_info</key>
        <dict>
                <key>pid</key>
                <string>98234573</string>
                <key>uid</key>
                <string>348576</string>
        </dict>
        <key>style</key>
        <string>fruit</string>
</dict>
</plist>
```

Notice that the key "cust_info" is a dictionary, rather than a simple, single value. PlistBuddy can easily update the values in this nested dictionary. PlistBuddy can also work interactively, which we won't cover here. You can, however, pass in all commands using the "-c" switch.

Here is an example: to set the value of a key, you need the path to the key and the "Set" command. The path to the key starts with a colon (":") and uses a colon as the separator for each level in the hierarchy. Here's how to change ("set") the value of the existing "pid" key to 94758476, in the file com.apress.example.plist:

```
/usr/libexec/PlistBuddy -c "Set :cust_info:pid 94758476" com.apress.example.plist
```

> **NOTE:** If you run PlistBuddy from a directory other than the one containing the .plist file you're manipulating, you'll need to specify the full path of the .plist file to edit.

See the PlistBuddy main page (note the capitalization) for more information on the utility. PlistBuddy is capable of much, much more, including copying values and merging .plist files.

Cocoa for Scripters

As alluded to earlier in this chapter, Apple's Cocoa framework has native methods for reading and writing property list files. Cocoa is exposed to Python, Ruby, and Perl via the *Objective-C bridge*.

While a full-out course on any of these scripting languages is beyond the scope of this book, we can give an overview for people who have some experience and just need examples of creating, writing, and reading .plist files.

Why, though, would you want to use a language like Ruby or Python instead of the other command-line tools (plutil, PlistBuddy, and, particularly, defaults) and bash scripting? From time to time, as a system administrator, you'll find yourself in a position where you'd like a script to store its own preferences. Or, you'd like to simply have a script analyze a .plist file and act on the contents in some manner. In many cases, bash scripting will be perfectly acceptable. However, for anything with a little more complexity, you may already be scripting in Python, Perl, or Ruby. While you can successfully use any of these, for demonstration purposes, we're going to use Python.

> **NOTE:** PyObjC is built into OS X 10.5 and above, and only with Python 2.5 and above. It's possible to use PyObjC with 10.4-based machines, but you'll need to compile and install PyObjC yourself. Mac OS X 10.5 ships with both Python 2.4 and 2.5, so be sure to stick with the default version of 2.5. Mac OS X 10.6 ships with both Python 2.5 and 2.6; both contain the Objective-C bridge support.

Python, with PyObjC (the Objective-C bridge), turns working with property list files into a pretty trivial operation. Most importantly, you get the best of both worlds: Apple's APIs, along with Python's ease of use and the speed of the edit and run cycle (skipping the compile step of C-based languages). To see this in action, let's start with nearly the simplest example possible. Listing 4-1 contains write_plist.py, which demonstrates creating a dictionary that gets written to a .plist file.

Listing 4-1. *write_plist.py*

```
#!/usr/bin/python2.5

from Foundation import NSMutableDictionary

my_dict = NSMutableDictionary.dictionary()

my_dict['color'] = 'blue'
my_dict['count'] = 15
my_dict['style'] = 'fruit'

success = my_dict.writeToFile_atomically_('com.apress.example.plist', 1)

if not success:
  print "plist failed to write!"
  sys.exit(1)
```

Upon running this program, `com.apress.example.plist` will be created in the same working directory as the program itself. The `.plist` file will match the output that is shown in Listing 4-1. Let's examine this line by line to see how it works.

The very first line—`#!/usr/bin/python2.5`—is a good reminder that Python version 2.5 or higher is required for PyObjC integration. This will not work on Tiger systems out of the box.

```
from Foundation import NSMutableDictionary
```

This import is responsible for all of the magic here. While we could import all of Foundation, we'll import just the portion we need: `NSMutableDictionary`.

```
my_dict = NSMutableDictionary.dictionary()
```

Typically, creating a dictionary in Python would use curly braces, like this:

```
new_dict = {}
```

Or, you can even fill it on creation:

```
new_dict = {'color':'blue', 'count':15, 'style':'fruit'}
```

However, we need to create a real Cocoa `NSMutableDictionary` object, so that's what we've done. Nicely, we can now go on and treat that just like a Python dictionary:

```
my_dict['color'] = 'blue'
my_dict['count'] = 15
my_dict['style'] = 'fruit'
```

You can use the Cocoa API for adding entries to a dictionary as well:

```
my_dict.setValue_forKey_('stop', 'state')
```

This would set the key "state" to store the value "stop," and add the following to the `.plist` file once written out:

```
<key>state</key>
<string>stop</string>
```

Honestly, though, if you're using Python, take advantage of it where you can! (I suggest using the Python method shown.) You will need to use the Cocoa API to write the dictionary out to disk as a `.plist` file:

```
success = my_dict.writeToFile_atomically_('com.apress.example.plist', 1)
```

The Cocoa `writeToFile:atomically:` method of `NSDictionary` (and, by extension, `NSMutableDictionary`) writes a property list representation of the contents of the dictionary to the path given.

```
if not success:
  print "plist failed to write!"
  sys.exit(1)
```

This final conditional tests to see if the `writeToFile:atomically:` method returned a true ("success") or false ("failure") value. While not strictly necessary for this program to run, checking these values is a good habit to get into.

Altering .plist Files in Memory

Once you create the NSMutableDictionary in memory, you can use standard Python mechanisms to manipulate and traverse it. Adding a key with a dictionary as its value is as simple as you'd expect. Just create the dictionary and then assign it to the parent dictionary. For example, to recreate `com.apress.example.plist` shown earlier, we would add the following to our program, after creating the initial dictionary:

```
sub_dict = {}
sub_dict['uid'] = '348576'
sub_dict['pid'] = '98234573'
my_dict['cust_info'] = sub_dict
```

Also, as shown earlier, you can also use all of the Cocoa APIs available to you to manipulate the dictionary as well. The style you choose may be situation-dependent. Some situations may call for using the Cocoa way, while others may favor more Pythonic writing. When working with any Cocoa API, though, as always, you'll want to keep the documentation handy.

Summary

Property list files, also known as ".plist" files because they use the .plist extension, are pervasive throughout the entire operating system. Managed Preferences are no exception to this and use the .plist format to store the preferences that you want to deliver to clients. If you plan to work with Managed Preferences, you should have a good understanding of what .plist files are, and the inner workings of the .plist format.

This chapter covered property list files in detail: what they are, where they reside, and ways to work with them. Apple provides built-in tools, both GUI-based and command-line-based, to manipulate property lists. Property List Editor is installed with Apple's Developer Tools. It provides a no-frills GUI that allows you to create and alter .plist files. There are several command-line tools that each have particular strengths for given tasks. The one you'll use most often is the defaults command, which allows alterations to .plist files in preference domains. Finally, we showed some sample Python code that creates a .plist file as a dictionary and then saves it to disk. We can't stress enough how much some basic scripting abilities will aid you as a system administrator, especially when dealing with file types that are native to the operating system.

Resources

NSDictionary Class Reference: http://developer.apple.com/mac/library/documentation/Cocoa/Reference/Foundation/Classes/NSDictionary_Class/Reference/Reference.html

Property List Programming Guide: http://developer.apple.com/mac/library/documentation/Cocoa/Conceptual/PropertyLists/Introduction/Introduction.html#//apple_ref/doc/uid/10000048i

## Chapter 5

Writing a Property List for Management

Now that you know what a property list file (".plist") is, what one should look like, and the basic tools for working with them, it's time to get more specific.

This chapter introduces the tools and methods used to create Managed Preferences. You'll learn what makes up a Managed Preferences .plist file, where this is stored, and how to get it there.

Managed Preferences rely on a directory service, and, therefore, these tools interact with a local or remote directory to enforce preferences. So, before delving into the tools themselves, let's first examine where Managed Preferences reside.

Where Do Managed Preferences Reside?

It's important to understand the location Managed Preferences call home. Managed Preferences work properly only if they're stored in the right place. If you're going to write a .plist file that will be used for management, where do you store it?

Apple's Managed Preferences rely on a directory service to work, which is why we gave an introduction to the topic in Chapter 3. Any directory that you work with will be laid out hierarchically, much like the file systems that you're used to. There's a root level that contains objects. (On a file system—ignoring files for now—these would be directories. In a directory service, these are typically organizational unit containers.) These objects can contain sub-objects. In both cases, you're allowed to use the structure to organize your data. When you're using Mac OS X, Apple has provided a structure that it expects to have available. Figure 5-1 shows a simplified and not fully complete sample directory tree.

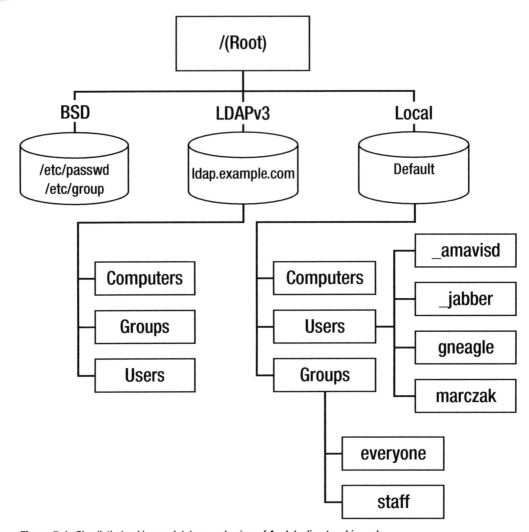

Figure 5-1. *Simplistic (and incomplete) example view of Apple's directory hierarchy*

In Figure 5-1, you'll note the root, represented by the forward slash character (/). Other branches of this tree descend from the root. In this diagram, the level just below the root represents the different directory service plug-ins—BSD, LDAP, and the local node. If a machine had Active Directory configured, it would appear here, too. Each of these branches can have other branches, and will ultimately end in *leaf nodes* or individual records. For example, under the path /Local/Default/Users are the user records for "_amavisd," "_jabberd," "gneagle," and "marczak." Each object in the hierarchy is either a container, or a record that resides in some specific container.

To further that point, the local record for the group staff would be said to be found at /Local/Default/Groups/staff. "staff" is the actual record. Each record is comprised of a set of attributes and values. Each record in a given container will be constructed from the same set of attributes. It's the values given to those attributes that make each record unique—like a record in a database. When we query the contents of this record ("staff"), we see the following attributes and values:

```
AppleMetaNodeLocation: /Local/Default
GeneratedUID: ABCDEFAB-CDEF-ABCD-EFAB-CDEF00000014
GroupMembers: AF54E0FF-7F61-A537-B51A-670997A5E774
GroupMembership: root
Password: *
PrimaryGroupID: 20
RealName: Staff
RecordName: staff
RecordType: dsRecTypeStandard:Groups
SMBSID: S-1-5-32-545
```

In this record, the value of "RecordName"—in other words, the group name—is "staff". Each group in Mac OS X gets a Generated UID associated with it, and this is stored in the "GeneratedUID" attribute. The PrimaryGroupID attribute is the glue between Apple's internal record-keeping and POSIX groups. However, there's only one thing to understand with respect to our needs: Managed Preferences (MCX) are just more attributes and values that get associated with a given record. There are two attributes needed: MCXFlags and MCXSettings.

The MCXFlags attribute simply alerts Mac OS X to the fact that this record has MCX data to be applied. The MCXSettings attribute contains the actual settings to be applied. Both attributes store these values as—you guessed it—property list files (.plist). The MCXSettings attribute in a record stores an XML-based .plist file containing the actual XML plists to be delivered to clients.

Preferred Tools for Creating, Testing, and Deploying Managed Preferences

We've already looked at utilities to help write a general .plist file. There are additional utilities that allow you to work with this .plist information in the context of the directory. Let's explore those now.

Using Workgroup Manager

Workgroup Manager is the easiest of the tools to use. As an Apple GUI tool, it basically just does the right thing. However, it's not solely a property list editor. As primarily a GUI for configuring users, groups and computers, It's not really much of a traditional editor at all. Workgroup Manager does know all about Managed Preferences, though.

> **NOTE:** If you haven't installed the Server Admin Tools as mentioned in Chapter 2, "What You'll Need," you'll need to do that to follow along in this chapter. Go download the installer and set yourself up now.

Creating a Property List File

Workgroup Manager.app is found in the /Applications/Server directory. Launch it now and you should be looking at a login dialog box similar to that shown in Figure 5-2.

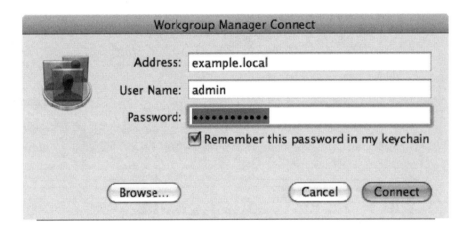

Figure 5-2. *Workgroup Manager sign-in dialog*

Don't worry—for our purposes you won't need to log in at all. To move forward here, click on the Server menu, and then choose the View Directories menu item. (Command-D is a shortcut for this menu command). Once done, you'll see a warning displayed, as shown in Figure 5-3.

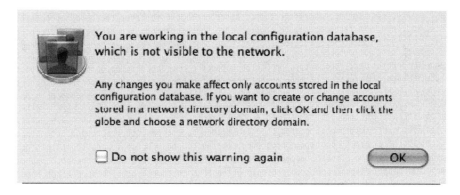

Figure 5-3. *Workgroup Manager local-only warning*

Since 5.30 Workgroup Manager is typically used to work on centralized, network-based directories, this warning is just letting you know that you're now looking at the local directory on your Macintosh. Despite Apple's intentions, this is exactly what we want right now, as we *do* want to be looking at the local "not-visible-to-the-network" directory. Since we're going to be doing this a fair amount, you may want to check the "Do not show this warning again" check box before clicking OK. Once you've cleared the warning, you'll be looking at the main Workgroup Manager window shown in Figure 5-4.

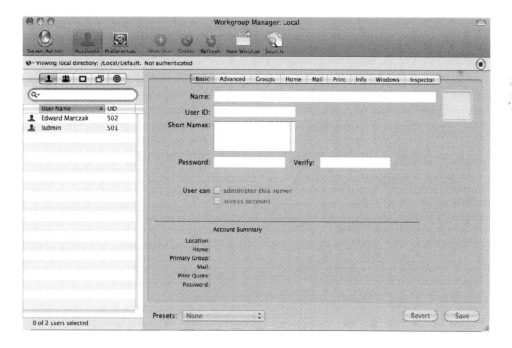

Figure 5-4. *Workgroup Manager's main window in its default state*

This window is divided into a toolbar across the top of the window, a left-side pane, and a right-side pane. The left-side pane represents the object that you've chosen from the tabs at the top of that pane representing a user, group, computer, or computer group object. The right-side pane will show the details of the operation you've chosen to perform from the toolbar (working with accounts or preferences).

If you've worked with OS X Server before, you've likely used Workgroup Manager and are familiar with this view. However, many people who use Workgroup Manager don't realize that it can be used to manage the local directory, too. For the purposes of our work in this book regarding Managed Preferences, we're concerned only with one area of Workgroup Manager: the Preferences section, accessed by clicking the "Preferences" button in the top toolbar. When you do so, the right-side pane will reveal the preferences panel (Figure 5-5).

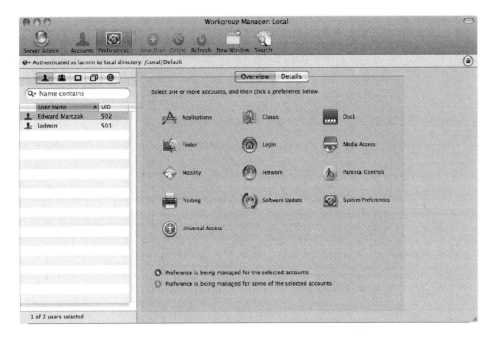

Figure 5-5. *Workgroup Manager's preference panel exposed*

Apple has categorized several different types of preferences on this panel that an admin would like to manage—you'll see them in the pane on the right ("Applications," "Classic," "Dock," and so on). However, you first need to choose the user, group, computer, or computer group you want the preferences applied to. For our purposes, choose a local user. When you click a category—for example, "Dock"—you'll be presented with a new panel that lists predefined preferences that Apple has chosen to expose for the selected category (Figure 5-6).

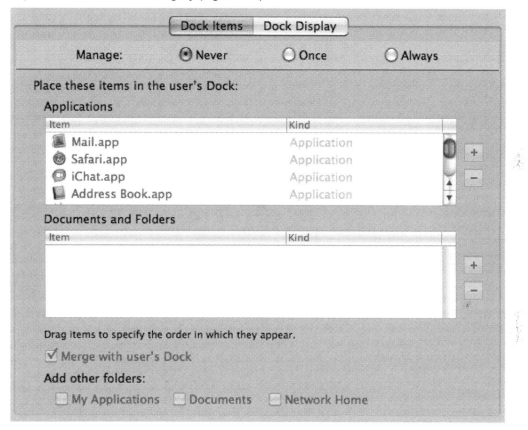

Figure 5-6. *Preferences for the Dock*

Initially, these preferences are grayed out. This is because you're not managing them; notice the status of "Manage" at the top of the pane—"Never" is selected. Chapter 8 will go deeper into the meanings of never, once, and always as they apply to Managed Preferences. For now, just select "Always" in order to inspect the offered preferences further. Click the "Dock Display" tab (you can see this tab in Figure 5-6). Notice that once you are viewing the "Dock Display" tab, that the preferences on each tab are managed separately and that you'll need to select "Always" again. Enable the check box for "Automatically Show and Hide the Dock" and click "Apply." There! You just wrote a .plist file for management!

Displaying the Inspector Tab

Apple's tools strive to make all of this simple. How, though, can you see what the GUI is actually doing to make this work? While this is generally good, geeky knowledge to have, we will need to take advantage of it when we want to have greater control over our preferences and simply do things the GUI can't on its own.

You'll need to ensure that you've configured Workgroup Manager to display the inspector tab. Choose "Preferences…" from the Workgroup Manager menu (Figure 5-4 shows the results of displaying the inspector tab) or you can press Command. Ensure that "Show 'All Records' tab and inspector" has a check mark next to it (Figure 5-7) and then click OK to close the dialog.

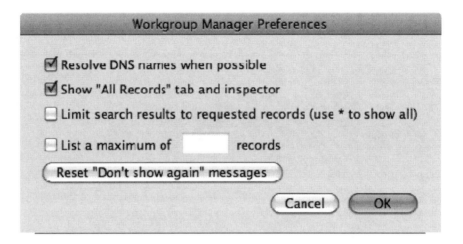

Figure 5-7. *Workgroup Manager Preferences*

This will add a "bulls-eye" tab to the tab-group of four tabs representing User, Group, Computer, and Computer group, making it five.

> **NOTE:** While we're looking at Workgroup Manager's preferences, let's examine an additional one. If you're in any kind of large environment—400 user accounts or more—you should take advantage of the "List a maximum of _____ records" preference. This stops Workgroup Manager from requesting the entire user list each time you launch the application and limits it to the count you specify. This speeds up Workgroup Manager's operations significantly, especially once you're around the threshold of 1,000 users and higher.
>
> If you do decide to implement this option, you'll need to search for the user record that you want to work with if it's outside the bounds of the count you've chosen. Simply start typing the name of the record into the "Name Contains" field directly above the record list.
>
> While this doesn't impact Managed Preferences in any way, it's useful to know about.

The inspector tab allows you to look at directory raw data records and edit them in place. Clicking the "Inspector" tab now will reveal a list that looks very much like that in Figure 5-8.

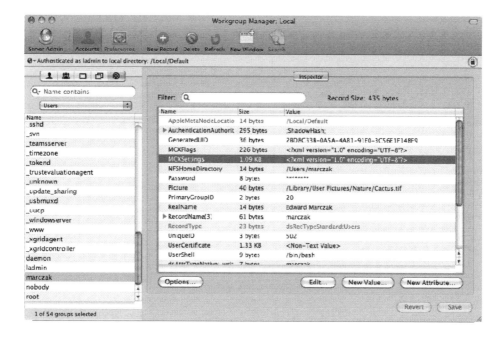

Figure 5-8. *Using Workgroup Manager's inspector tab to look at raw directory data*

Ensure that the drop-down menu displays the type of directory record you're looking for, and choose the object. You should find a record named "MCXSettings." Highlight that record and click the "Edit…" button underneath the list of attributes. The screen in Figure 5-9 will appear.

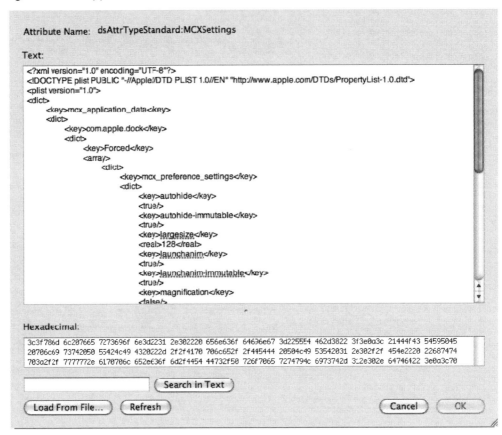

Figure 5-9. *Editing the value of a directory record attribute in Workgroup Manager*

Ah ha! This is the result of our earlier work in the pure-GUI portion of Workgroup Manager: it *did* write an XML .plist file. It takes that .plist file and writes it to a record in the directory. Better yet, you can *edit* it here, too. This includes copy and paste. If you're using a third-party directory to manage your Mac OS X machines, and have extended the schema of its directory with the Apple extensions, don't ignore Workgroup Manager as a utility. You can still create your preferences using Workgroup Manager, inspect the raw data, copy it, and then paste it into the directory that your machines are actually bound to.

NOTE: Speaking of directories, the directory you're using likely has an LDAP interface. This includes Apple's Open Directory, Microsoft's Active Directory, OpenLDAP, and others. If you're an advanced user, you may be tempted to use the `ldapsearch` command or other LDAP tools to reach into the directory and manipulate MCX data. The Apple tools actually encode and decode MCX data as needed, so you may not be successful. Outside of the `ldapmodify` command, to get a blob of information into a record, the standard array of `ldap` commands will be of little use when it comes to MCX attributes.

Often, you'll need to get at these raw property lists in order to manage third-party, "non-Apple" preferences.

Managing Non-Apple Preferences

As shown earlier in Figure 5-5, Workgroup Manager has many predefined categories of preferences. Inherently, though, these categories are limiting. Only the preferences that Apple thought to display are exposed (purposefully or otherwise). Additionally, there are many non-Apple preferences that you may want to manage. Thankfully, Apple *did* include a way to handle this.

As mentioned in Chapter 4, preferences are part and parcel of Mac OS X's user defaults system. A well-behaved application will use the proper programming interface to save preferences according to Apple's guidelines and not come up with a new scheme of the developer's choosing. Fortunately, most every modern application will actually conform to the user defaults method. How do we allow Workgroup Manager to work with these non-Apple preferences? After choosing an object to set preferences for and clicking the "Preferences" button in the toolbar (shown earlier in Figure 5-5), the default view presents the "Overview" panel. Choosing the "Details" tab on this panel reveals a way to add arbitrary preferences (Figure 5-10).

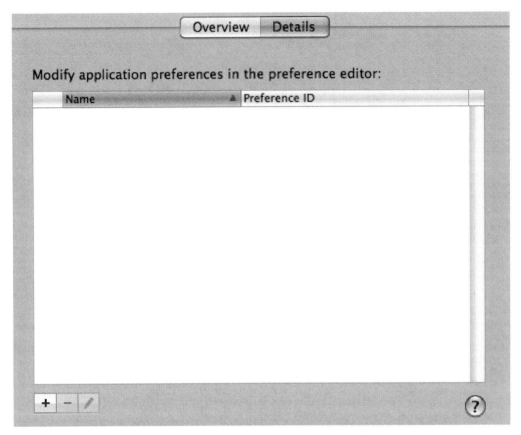

Figure 5-10. *Workgroup Manager's preference details tab allows you to add arbitrary preferences.*

Using the Preference Details view, you can import preferences from any application that stores its preferences in the standard Apple .plist format. This includes third-party applications.

We'll delve into this topic in more depth in Chapter 9, and Chapter 10, "Recipes," contains several concrete examples that should solidify this for you.

The dscl Command

The dscl command—short for "directory service command line"—is the command-line equivalent of Workgroup Manager. Some steps may be a bit more tedious, but there certainly is one huge advantage that dscl has over Workgroup Manager: the ability to be used in a script and automated. Of course, that doesn't mean you should ignore Workgroup Manager in favor of dscl; they complement each other nicely.

Originally introduced in Mac OS X 10.4, as of Mac OS X 10.5, the dscl utility gained specific extensions to handle MCX data. This coincided with another change in moving from 10.4 to 10.5: gone is the proprietary Apple-only NeXT-holdover of the NetInfo directory that existed prior to 10.5, replaced with the current local directory service based on open XML .plist files. dscl is your command-line interface to this directory. Let's look at how this command can be used to manipulate directory information.

Choosing a Directory to Work with

The dscl command can list a directory container using the list command. This works with the local directory, or any directory Mac OS X can bind to, such as Open Directory, generic LDAP, or Active Directory. In any case, you need to specify which directory you're trying to work with. For example, to list all user records in the local directory in the default node, use the list command like this:

```
dscl /Local/Default list /Users
```

Notice that we need to specify the directory, then the command (list) and the container that we want to list. The full path to the container must be specified relative to the base directory that you supply. Similarly, if your Mac is bound to an Open Directory server, the command would need to specify that remote directory:

```
dscl /LDAPv3/server.example.com list /Groups
```

There's a shortcut to specifying the local default node: the "." character. Our original list example command could be rewritten like this:

```
dscl . list /Users
```

We'll be using this shortcut for any further examples that reference the local default directory.

To read a specific record in a container, use the read command:

```
$ dscl . read /Users/root
AppleMetaNodeLocation: /Local/Default
GeneratedUID: FFFFEEEE-DDDD-CCCC-BBBB-AAAA00000000
NFSHomeDirectory: /var/root
Password: *
PrimaryGroupID: 0
RealName:
 System Administrator
RecordName: root
RecordType: dsRecTypeStandard:Users
SMBSID: S-1-5-18
UniqueID: 0
UserShell: /bin/sh
```

It's also possible to read one single attribute from a record. Specify the attribute after the record name:

```
$ dscl /Local/Default read /Users/marczak RealName
RealName:
 Edward R. Marczak
```

The dscl command can also be used to add an attribute/value pair to a record by creating it:

```
$ sudo dscl . create /Users/mike flagged 1
Password:
$ dscl . read /Users/mike flagged
dsAttrTypeNative:flagged: 1
```

One perfect use for this in relation to Managed Preferences is to create a record for the local machine in order to apply preferences to it.

```
sudo dscl . -create /Computers/local_computer
sudo dscl . -create /Computers/local_computer RealName "Local Computer"
sudo dscl . -create /Computers/local_computer GeneratedUID $(uuidgen)
sudo dscl . -create /Computers/local_computer ENetAddress $(ifconfig en0 | awk /ether/
'{print $2}')
sudo dscl . -create /Computers/local_computer IPAddress 127.0.0.1
```

First, we create the record "local_computer." From there, we create the attributes "RealName," "GeneratedUID," "ENetAddress," and "IPAddress," and fill them with appropriate values—values specific to this machine. This is a great example of a task that would be completely manual with Workgroup Manager but is able to be automated using dscl.

> **NOTE:** If you're going to be automating tasks with `dscl` and checking exit codes (*as you should*), not everything works as you may expect. Most obvious errors return a non-zero exit code:
>
> [~]$ dscl . list /User ; echo $?
>
> list: Invalid Path
>
> <dscl_cmd> DS Error: -14009 (eDSUnknownNodeName)
>
> 185
>
> [~]$ dscl . read /Users/missinguser ; echo $?
>
> <dscl_cmd> DS Error: -14136 (eDSRecordNotFound)
>
> 56
>
> However, an unknown attribute in a record is not considered an error, apparently:
>
> [~]$ dscl . read /Users/marczak MISSINGATTRIBUTE ; echo $?
>
> No such key: MISSINGATTRIBUTE
>
> 0
>
> It's something to be very aware of. You may need to employ more parsing to get useful results.

Working with MCX

Since we know that our managed preferences are just another attribute—named MCXSettings—we can certainly use `dscl read` to read its value:

```
dscl . read /Computers/guest MCXSettings
```

However, as mentioned, beginning with Mac OS X 10.5, `dscl` has MCX-specific extensions. Let's take a look at those.

Even as of Mac OS X 10.6.3, the MCX extensions to `dscl` are conspicuously absent from `dscl`'s main page. You can get fairly detailed help, however, by using the -mcxhelp switch:

```
dscl . -mcxhelp
```

Note that you still need to supply a directory with the –mcxhelp switch, even though you're not operating on any directory. The local directory is represented in the example above by the "." between the `dscl` command and the "-mcxhelp" switch.

How do these extensions help you over the base set of `dscl` commands?

The MCX commands are largely convenience functions, though they shine a light on the actual nature of the records they're working with. There are six functions available to help you with MCX: `mcxread`, `mcxset`, `mcxedit`, `mcxdelete`, `mcxexport`, and `mcximport`.

The `mcxread` command does what you'd expect: present you with the attributes and values that make up the MCXSettings attribute in a given record. It also gives some information regarding those attributes. Take a look at an example:

```
dscl . mcxread /Computers/guest com.apple.sidebarlists
Key: networkbrowser
State: often
Value: {
    Controller = CustomListItems;
    CustomListProperties =    {
        "com.apple.NetworkBrowser.backToMyMacEnabled" = 1;
        "com.apple.NetworkBrowser.bonjourEnabled" = 1;
        "com.apple.NetworkBrowser.connectedEnabled" = 1;
    };
}
```

The `mcxset` command provides an easy way to set MCX values for a given record. For example, to set the Dock's display type to the 2D non-glass look for an entire computer, set the value in MCX for the local_computer computer record (see previous instructions on how to create the local_computer computer record):

```
sudo dscl . mcxset /Computers/local_computer com.apple.dock no-glass always -boolean
true
```

Note the use of `sudo` in this command, as writing into the directory is a privileged operation. For the local directory, we use `sudo`. For a remote directory, you would need to provide credentials that have write access. `dscl` provides the -u flag for this. This example shows you how:

```
dscl -u adminuser /LDAPv3/ldap.example.com mcxset /Computers/localhost com.apple.dock
no-glass always -boolean true
```

The `mcxedit` command allows you to update the value of a preference key without disturbing the rest of the MCX setting. For example, if the Dock's autohide preference key is already being managed for the local_computer object, the following command would edit that value:

```
sudo dscl . mcxedit /Computers/localhost com.apple.dock autohide -bool 1
```

If you try to edit a key that doesn't exist, `dscl` will exit with a code of 64 and print to standard error, "Key does not already exist."

`mcxdelete` will delete a single preference key from a given preference domain. It's effectively the opposite of `mcxset`. For example, if you no longer wanted to manage the Dock autohide setting for the local_computer object, the following command would remove that setting:

```
sudo dscl . mcxdelete /Computers/local_computer com.apple.dock autohide
```

`mcxexport` and `mcximport` allow you to store and reapply entire preference settings. While similar to `mcxread`, `mcxexport` will allow the MCX record to be stored as a `.plist` file of a given type. The output of `mcxexport` is also ready to be imported using `mcximport`. In some ways, this is analogous to copying and pasting MCX settings between records in Workgroup Manager. This even works between directories. Let's look at an example.

If you've been testing settings on a local machine and are ready to use these settings for all computers bound to a centralized, network-based directory, there's no need to recreate this configuration from scratch. First, export the values from the local directory:

```
dscl . mcxexport /Computers/local_computer -o comp_settings.plist
```

This will export a plain text `.plist` file of all MCX settings applied to the local_computer object from the local directory. This is a great opportunity to store this `.plist` file of values in your company's version control system. (You are using version control, right?) From there, we can import these preferences into another directory. For example, if your central directory is Microsoft's Active Directory and you (or your Active Directory administrator) have extended the schema, you could import it with this command:

```
dscl -u adminuser mcximport /ActiveDirectory/Computers -o comp_settings.plist
```

This is an incredible way to store and set Managed Preferences. Prior to adding these subcommands to `dscl`, it was difficult to perform any of this. Now, we have a way to manage the `.plist` files that make up our preferences. One possible workflow for creating, storing, and deploying a single managed preference could look like this:

1. Use Workgroup Manager to create a new preference. This preference doesn't need to be created on a specific machine—all you need is Workgroup Manager.

2. Export the preference using `dscl -mcxexport`. Once exported, this XML snippet can be stored outside of any directory service; it can be stored in a version control system. This is a way to ensure consistency and verify changes.

3. The exported preference can now be imported using `dscl -mcximport` into the appropriate record in any properly configured directory service.

The `mcx` commands added to `dscl` are a welcome improvement.

The defaults Command Refresher

The `defaults` command was covered in depth in Chapter 4. This section serves as a reminder and way to reinforce how the `defaults` command interacts with our preferences and how it can be used.

The `defaults` command is used to alter `.plist`-based preference files in a given user defaults domain. Managed Preferences also interact in this space. If you're just formulating ideas for a Managed Preferences control, using the `defaults` command to set a value locally is useful for testing. From there, you may want to examine the `.plist` file in order to copy the `.plist`-formatted information to be used in Workgroup Manager or set via a `dscl mcxset` command.

Do note, though, that if you're already using Managed Preferences on a given machine, the MCX controls put in place will outrank the values set with `defaults` if there's a clash in a given preference. This is, of course, as it should be. Chapter 7 will contain more information on this order of rules.

Summary

This chapter introduced tools to manage property lists for Managed Preferences. Workgroup Manager is an optional, Apple-supplied utility intended to manage a Mac OS X Server. It works nicely to manage preferences for the local directory, too. The command-line equivalent to Workgroup Manager is `dscl`—the directory services command line. Its major advantages over Workgroup Manager are its speed and that it can be scripted.

## Chapter 6

Delivering Managed Preferences

In the previous chapter, you saw how to create preferences and how to store them in a directory. But how do you deliver the preferences to the client machine being managed?

In this chapter, you'll learn about several ways to deliver these preferences. Depending on your environment, you may use just one of these techniques, or a combination of them all. We'll start with the common case of using Apple's own Open Directory running on Mac OS X Server. From there, we'll introduce Microsoft's Active Directory as a way to manage your Macs.

Finally, we'll show you ways to deliver Managed Preferences even in the case where you don't have a centralized directory service available to you for the purpose of storing MCX data.

Directory Choices

In this chapter, we'll talk about several different centralized directory services to use in conjunction with delivering Managed Preferences. We'll specifically talk about the following:

- Apple's Open Directory
- Microsoft's Active Directory
- OpenLDAP

We're covering these particular directory services as they're some of the most prevalent, but ideally, you can use any directory service that is accessible over LDAP, or one that has a plug-in for Open Directory. The trick is in the configuration of the service and binding of the client machines. Once that step is done, each directory service is largely equal.

Delivery with Open Directory

Delivering Managed Preferences inside an all-Apple environment largely just works. It's all as Apple intended it: an easy to use GUI creates preferences and delivers them to bound machines. This is the case where you have an end-to-end Mac OS X environment: Mac OS X Server running Open Directory and your Mac OS X client machines. The first thing to do is bind the clients to the server.

Binding Mac OS X Clients to Open Directory

Binding a computer to a directory service is the process of associating that computer with a directory. This association connects the client machine so it is able to look up resources in the directory automatically. It uses this information for local authentication, group information, and more.

It's beyond the scope of this book to detail every way possible to bind your clients to Open Directory. We'd be remiss, though, if we didn't detail any, so we'll show the basic GUI method of binding to Open Directory. Under Mac OS X 10.6, these steps are easy:

1. Open the Accounts preferences pane from System Preferences->Accounts.

2. Authenticate by clicking the lock icon in the lower left corner if necessary.

3. Click the "Login Options" tab and then the "Join…" button (highlighted in Figure 6-1).

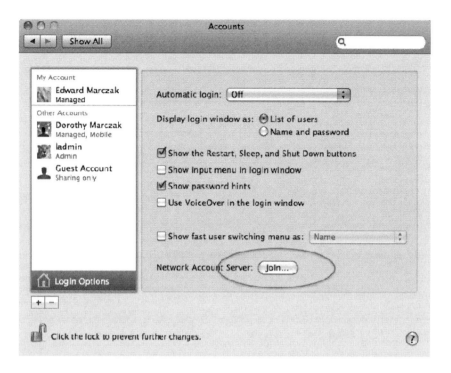

Figure 6-1. *The Accounts preferences pane provides the entry point to binding.*

4. Provide the fully qualified DNS name of the Open Directory server in the resulting dialog box.

5. The client machine and the server will configure settings and perform the binding. Once complete, you'll see the successful binding reflected in the resulting Directory Server sheet. Look for the green light in the upper left corner. In the case of Figure 6-2, it appears to the left of "abyss.rdiotope.com."

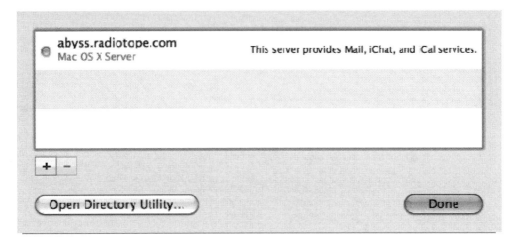

Figure 6-2. *Directory Service sheet showing an active binding to an Open Directory server*

In an all-Apple environment, that's pretty much it. From here, you can launch Workgroup Manager on this machine to ensure that you can access network resources.

Accessing the Directory

At the initial Workgroup Manager authentication dialog, supply the name of the Open Directory server and credentials that have administrative rights in that directory. Browse the data in the User and Group tabs. You should be seeing data from the server, as shown in Figure 6-3.

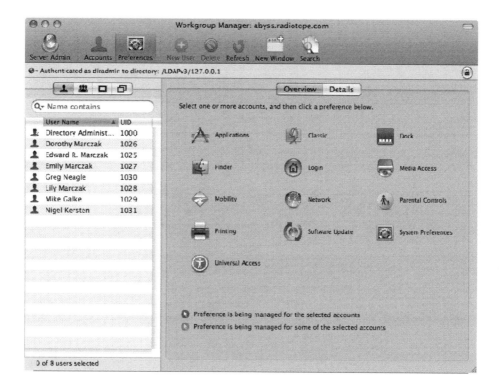

Figure 6-3. *Viewing network data via Workgroup Manager*

Notice that Workgroup Manager lists the directory you're viewing. In this case, we've "Authenticated as diradmin to directory /LDAPv3/127.0.0.1."

From this point, you can create managed preferences for user, group, computer, or computer group records using the techniques shown in the rest of this book. While we'd prefer that you keep reading straight through, if you're really anxious, feel free to try some of the recipes in Chapter 10.

Delivery with Active Directory

Microsoft's Active Directory ("AD") presents an interesting opportunity—one that Apple needed to take advantage of. In an environment with any investment in Active Directory, it's unlikely that a company will just rip out Windows servers and replace them with Mac OS X Server just for the sake of client management. Fortunately, there's no need.

Apple debuted the Active Directory plug-in for Open Directory in Mac OS X 10.3. Working with the plug-in in its early incarnations was imperfect at best. However, those days are gone, and, as of the writing of this book, working with Active Directory from Mac OS X 10.6 is a breeze.

> **NOTE:** Sometimes, I believe the Active Directory plug-in gets more attention than some of Apple's native tools. It's that good. In some ways, that makes sense: Apple's entry into the enterprise isn't going to be in supplying servers, but rather in making Mac OS X the best client on the planet. Being a good client means working well with others.

Binding Mac OS X Clients to Active Directory

To manage Mac OS X with Active Directory alone, each Mac will need to be bound to Active Directory.

Binding to Active Directory is simple: open Directory Utility.app, either directly from /System/Library/CoreServices, or via the Accounts preferences pane (you'll need to click "Login Options" and then the "Network Account Server" button). Authenticate with an admin-level account and then double-click the "Active Directory" entry. Provide the information requested and click OK.

> **NOTE:** We fully realize that the information that one must provide to the Active Directory plug-in will differ based on environment. However, the plug-in does a great job of figuring out how it needs to bind even with the most basic of information in all but a few cases. Those cases tend to be complex multi-forest setups. If this is your case, there's also likely a dedicated Windows or Active Directory administrator that can help you with the correct values for the plug-in. Keep in mind that binding a Mac OS X computer to Active Directory means that it will use that directory for not only preferences, but also authentication information.

Once bound, you'll find a host of options. However, if you try to use any centralized managed preferences, you won't get very far. If you load up Workgroup Manager as shown earlier, and try to use the Preferences tab, you'll be greeted with a dialog like that in Figure 6-4.

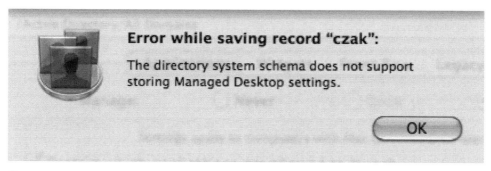

Error while saving record "czak":

The directory system schema does not support storing Managed Desktop settings.

OK

Figure 6-4. *Attempting to set preferences for the user "czak" in Active Directory*

Since Mac OS X—even ones bound to Active Directory—does not utilize Group Policy (the Windows equivalent to Managed Preferences), we need a way to implement the "Apple way" with Active Directory alone. The solution for this is to extend Active Directory's schema so it can hold the Apple attributes necessary for Managed Preferences. If you're a Mac-only person, you may want to find and hire someone who can help you with this process. If you're a Windows admin, you're either already familiar with this, or have always wanted to try it (right?).

> **NOTE:** Before we go further, modifying *any* directory service schema can have potentially bad consequences. This shouldn't dissuade you from doing so. However, testing and a proper rollback plan are critical. Again, if this is your first time using these tools, you may want to hire someone who can help with the process. If not, practice, practice, practice until fear turns to boredom.

In the next section, we walk you through the basic steps of extending the schema. Like the Active Directory plug-in itself, the tools that exist for this now are much better than they once were.

> **NOTE:** We performed this procedure using the latest operating systems available to us at the time: Mac OS X Server 10.6.3 and Microsoft Windows Server 2008 R2. Earlier versions of Windows introduce slight variations. Future versions of either system may also have differences. Be aware of this.

Extending the Active Directory Schema

Each directory service contains a map of the attributes it supports, called a *schema*. Apple's schema for Open Directory contains all of the attributes needed to support Managed Preferences. On the other hand, by default, Microsoft's Active Directory does not contain any room for these attributes. The Active Directory schema maps out attributes that are important only to Windows clients. Like any good directory service, though, the Active Directory schema can be extended. Specifically, you need to add the Apple attributes for management. This also involves creating and importing an LDAP Data Interchange Format (LDIF) file that will ultimately be imported into Active Directory to extend the AD schema, which we show you here as well. Microsoft provides all of the tools that you'll need to perform this task. You'll also need an Open Directory server, your Windows Server, and the Windows Active Directory Application Mode tools. (If you don't have a Mac OS X Server running Open Directory, beg or borrow one. If that doesn't work, we have sample files for you at http://mcxbook.com.)

Adding Apple's Attributes

To begin with, you'll need to log in to your master Active Directory controller. (Actually, to begin with, you should have a good night's rest, a clear mind, and full stomach. *Then* you'll need to log in to your master controller.) If not already configured, install the Lightweight Directory Services (LDS) role on the master controller. This installs the Active Directory Application Mode (ADAM) tools. From there, follow these steps.

1. Run C:\Windows\ADAM\ADSchemaAnalyzer.exe. You should then see this ugly-looking LDAP icon:

   Double-click it to launch the LDAP Schema Analyzer tool.

2. In the schema analyzer, choose File->Load Target Schema. This allows us to load the schema from another LDAP server. In this case, we're going to point it to our server running Open Directory. (If you don't have an Open Directory Server *anywhere*, you can download our Mac OS X Server 10.6.3 Schema from http://mcxbook.com and choose "Load LDIF..." in the Load Target Schema dialog. Really, though, it's best to actually perform this step.)

3. Fill in the IP address of the Open Directory Server (Figure 6-5). Leave the Username and Password fields empty and ensure that the Bind type parameter is set to "Simple."

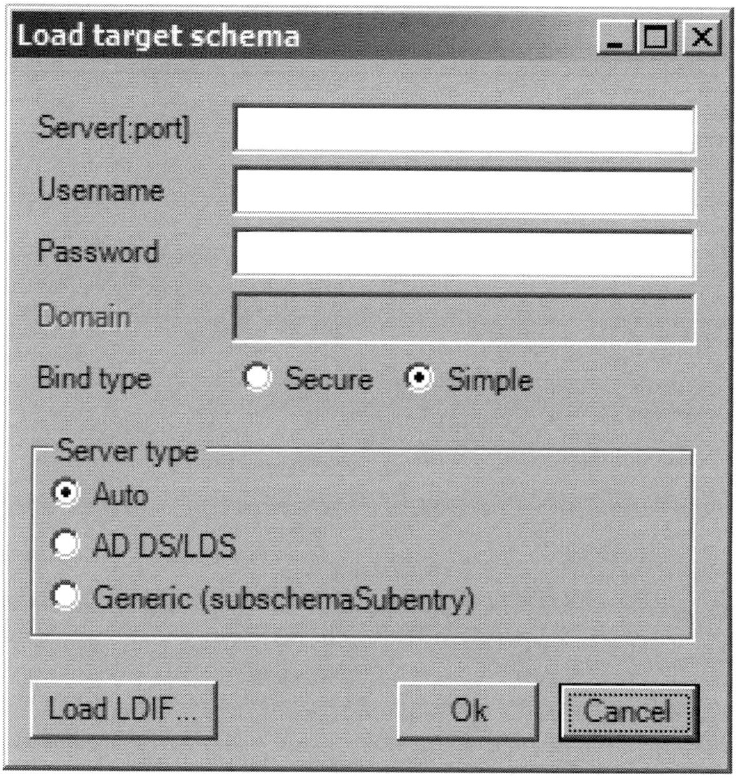

Figure 6-5. *Loading a target schema into the Schema Analyzer tool*

4. Click OK and the utility will import the schema from your Open Directory server. The main window will populate with Classes, Attributes, and Property Sets containers, as shown in Figure 6-6.

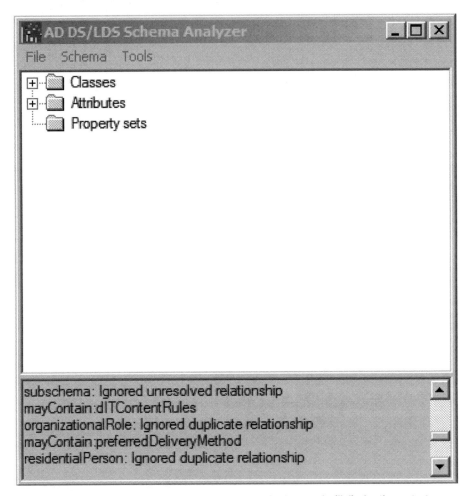

Figure 6-6. *After loading the target schema, the Schema Analyzer tool will display the contents.*

5. Choose File->Load Base Schema. Now that the target schema is loaded, we can compare it to a baseline in order to find the differences between the two.

6. The Load Base Schema dialog box is the same as the Load Target Schema dialog (Figure 6-5). Unlike the first run-through, where we targeted Open Directory, we're going to point it at our Active Directory master controller. Fill in the Server field with your Active Directory domain. Fill in the Username and Password fields with credentials that have the ability to read the entire schema. (This is typically your "administrator" account, but in many cases, an Active Directory admin will change this. Talk to your Active Directory admin if you are unsure what to use here.)

7. Change the Bind type to "Secure" and the Server type to "AD DS/LDS," and then click OK.

8. Choose Schema->Hide Present Elements. This will hide elements that match between the two directories, but still display only elements that differ.

9. Expand the Classes container. The class attributes will be displayed, as shown in Figure 6-7.

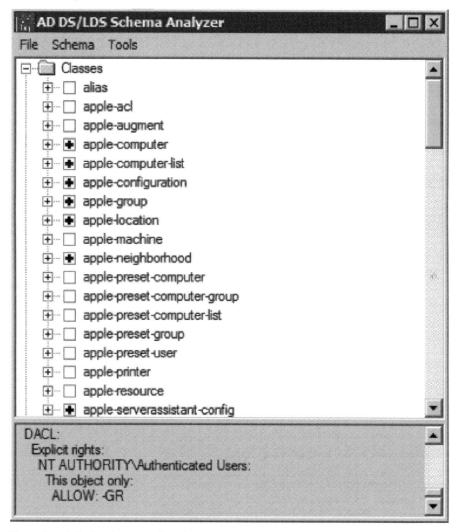

Figure 6-7. *Selecting the appropriate classes*

10. Select the following classes (place a plus sign in each check box):

apple-computer

apple-computer-list

apple-configuration

apple-group

apple-location

apple-neighborhood

apple-serverassistant-config

apple-service

apple-user

mount

11. Expand each class that you selected, and *enable* the following while *disabling* all other attributes (ensure there's a black X in the check box, as shown in Figure 6-8):

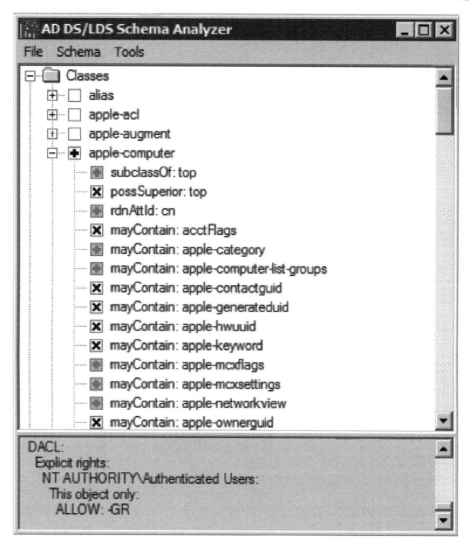

Figure 6-8. *Selecting the attributes that will be used to extend the AD schema*

apple-computer

  subclassOf: top

  rdnAttId: cn

  mayContain: apple-category

  mayContain: apple-computer-list-groups

  mayContain: apple-keyword apple-mcxflags

mayContain: apple-mcxsettings

mayContain: apple-networkview

mayContain: apple-service-url

mayContain: apple-xmlplist

mayContain: macAddress

mayContain: ttl

apple-computer-list

  subclassOf: top

  rdnAttId: cn

  mayContain: apple-computer-list-groups

  mayContain: apple-computers

  mayContain: apple-keyword

  mayContain: apple-mcxflags

  mayContain: apple-mcxsettings

apple-configuration

  subclassOf: top

  rdnAttId: cn

  mayContain: apple-data-stamp

  mayContain: apple-keyword

  mayContain: apple-xmlplist

  mayContain: ttl

apple-group

  subclassOf: top

  rdnAttId: cn

  mayContain: apple-group-homeowner

  mayContain: apple-group-homeurl

  mayContain: apple-keyword

  mayContain: apple-mcxflags

mayContain: apple-mcxsettings

mayContain: apple-user-picture

mayContain: ttl

apple-location

  subclassOf: top

  rdnAttId: cn

  mayContain: apple-dns-domain

  mayContain: apple-dns-nameserver

apple-neighborhood

  subclassOf: top

  rdnAttId: cn

  mayContain: apple-category

  mayContain: apple-computeralias

  mayContain: apple-keyword

  mayContain: apple-neighborhoodalias

  mayContain: apple-nodepathxml

  mayContain: apple-xmlplist

  mayContain: ttl

apple-serverassistant-config

  subclassOf: top

  rdnAttId: cn

  mayContain: apple-xmlplist

apple-service

  subclassOf: top

  rdnAttId: cn

  mayContain: apple-dnsname

  mayContain: apple-keyword

mayContain: apple-service-location

mayContain: apple-service-port

mayContain: apple-service-url

mayContain: ipHostNumber

mustContain: apple-service-type

apple-user

subclassOf: top

rdnAttId: cn

mayContain: apple-imhandle

mayContain: apple-keyword

mayContain: apple-mcxflags

mayContain: apple-mcxsettings

mayContain: apple-user-authenticationhint

mayContain: apple-user-class

mayContain: apple-user-homequota

mayContain: apple-userhomesoftquota

mayContain: apple-user-mailattribute

mayContain: apple-user-picture

mayContain: apple-user-printattribute

mayContain: apple-webloguri

mount

subclassOf: top

rdnAttId: cn

mayContain: mountDirectory

mayContain: mountDumpFrequency

mayContain: mountOption

mayContain: mountPassNo

mayContain: mountType

Now we need to create an LDIF file to be imported into Active Directory.

Creating an LDIF File

Follow these steps.

1. Choose File->Create LDIF. This creates an LDIF file ("LDAP Data Interchange Format") that will ultimately be imported into Active Directory to extend the AD schema. Save the file under any name you wish. We'll use "MCX_in_AD_Extensions.ldif."

2. After exporting the file, ensure that the information portion of the main window reports that the LDIF file was created with "36 attributes, 10 classes, 0 property sets, 0 updated present elements" (Figure 6-9). If you have more or less than any of these figures, stop here, double-check your selections, and export the file again.

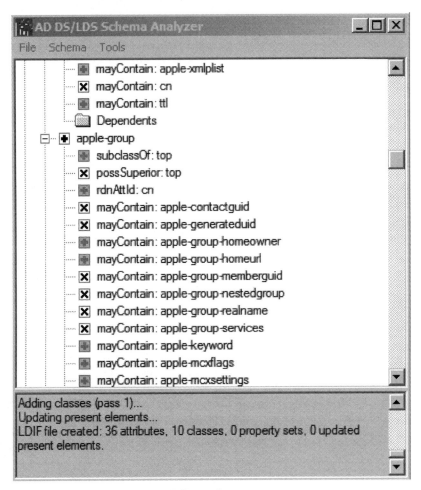

Figure 6-9. *Report of successful LDIF file creation*

3. Load the resulting LDIF file into Wordpad (Figure 6-10). An LDIF file is simply text. The exported LDIF file is largely correct; however, there are some changes that we need to make.

> **NOTE:** Because an LDIF is just text, you could copy the LDIF file we're working with back to your Macintosh to make the upcoming changes and use any text editor that you're comfortable with. You'll need to copy it back to the server when finished, though.

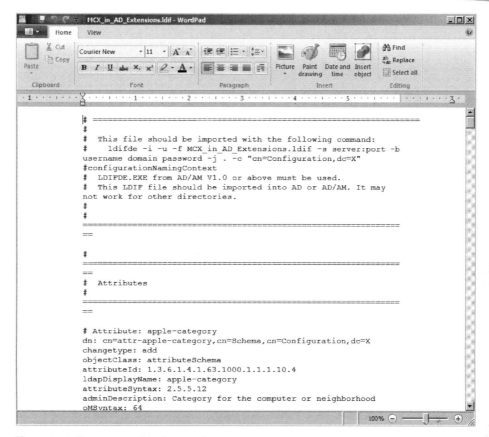

Figure 6-10. *The exported LDIF displayed in Wordpad*

4.   In the definition for the following objectClasses, change the objectClassCategory to "3" (it will be "0"): apple-user, apple-group, and apple-computer. This defines the object class as one that extends current information in the schema. Since user, group, and computer types already exist in Active Directory's schema, we just need to extend it, and not create it.

5.   Save the file you're working on, just to be safe.

6.   Add the following lines to the very end of the LDIF file, in the section labeled "Updating present elements":

```
dn: CN=User,CN=Schema,CN=Configuration,DC=X

changetype: modify

add: auxiliaryClass

auxiliaryClass: apple-user

-


CN=Computer,CN=Schema,CN=Configuration,DC=X

changetype: modify

add: auxiliaryClass

auxiliaryClass: apple-computer

-


CN=Group,CN=Schema,CN=Configuration,DC=X

changetype: modify

add: auxiliaryClass

auxiliaryClass: apple-group

-
```

NOTE: The formatting of these lines is important. The single-line hyphens are a correct part of the file. Although you can't easily see it in print, a return character is required after each hyphen, including the very last one. If this final return character is not present, the LDIF file will fail to import properly.

7. These additional lines allow our changes to be associated with the correct object classes in Active Directory. Save the file you're working on.

8. Remove unnecessary attribute prefixes. As a convenience, the ADSchemaAnalyzer prefixes our attributes with "attr-" and all classes with "cls". This is unnecessary, though, as everything we've imported already has a prefix of "apple-".

9. Across the entire document, search for "cn=cls-" and replace it with "cn=".

10. Across the entire document, search for "cn=attr-" and replace it with "cn=".

11. Only one class that we imported did not have any vendor-specific prefix. The mount object class needs to have the "apple-" prefix added.

12. Alter the mount record so it contains the following entries (prefixing each cn with "apple-"):

```
dn: cn=apple-mountDirectory,cn=Schema,cn=Configuration,dc=X
dn: cn=apple-mountDumpFrequency,cn=Schema,cn=Configuration,dc=X
dn: cn=apple-mountOption,cn=Schema,cn=Configuration,dc=X
dn: cn=apple-mountPassNo,cn=Schema,cn=Configuration,dc=X
dn: cn=apple-mountType,cn=Schema,cn=Configuration,dc=X
dn: cn=apple-mount,cn=Schema,cn=Configuration,dc=X
```

13. Define parent objects. For the object classes that we're creating, we need to define their parent, or, "superior" container objects. Add the following lines to the following classes:

```
possSuperiors: organizationalUnit
possSuperiors: container
```

apple-computer-list

apple-configuration

apple-location

apple-neighborhood

apple-serverassistant-config

apple-service

apple-mount

14. Save the LDIF file one final time.

15. Update the Active Directory schema.

Now our LDIF file is ready, and we can import it into Active Directory.

Importing the LDIF File

Open a Command Prompt, change the directory into the same directory that contains the MCX_in_AD_Extensions.ldif file and run the following command:

```
ldifde /j . /k /i /f MCX_in_AD_Extensions.ldif /v /c "DC=X"
"DC=Controller,DC=Server,DC=com"
```

You'll see some informational output initially, followed by each entry being modified:

```
Connecting to "WIN-KVCKKOI3VEC.bucsden.radiotope.com"
Logging in as current user using SSPI
Importing directory from file "MCX_in_AD_Extensions.ldif"
Loading entries
```

...output removed for brevity...

```
51 entries modified successfully.

The command has completed successfully
```

That's it!

> **NOTE:** Is that really it? Well, possibly not. Each Macintosh is identified by its Ethernet MAC address. This is what will be used for searching LDAP. If you have only a handful of machines, you're done. However, if you ever plan on growing the number of machines in Active Directory or already have a large deployment, the "macAddress" attribute should be indexed for faster lookups. Microsoft has a knowledge-base article on indexing attributes in AD here: http://technet.microsoft.com/en-us/library/aa995762(EXCHG.65).aspx.

Managing Preferences in Active Directory

Once the Active Directory schema is extended, *now* you'll be able to use Workgroup Manager—or any of the other methods we present—to alter MCX within Active Directory no differently than you would for a network-based Open Directory or local directory node. However, you'll need to perform these actions from a Macintosh that is bound to Active Directory.

When you launch Workgroup Manager, you'll need to ignore the request to authenticate and choose Server->View Directories. Alternatively, just press command-D when presented with the authentication dialog.

Choose the target directory by clicking the globe icon, as shown in Figure 6-11.

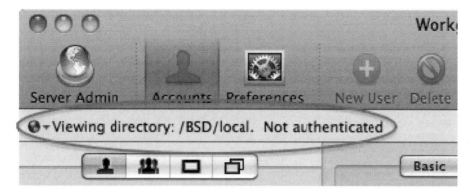

Figure 6-11. *Clicking the globe icon presents a drop-down menu of target directories.*

Choose "Active Directory/All Domains" from the menu (or pick it from "Other…" if necessary). Then click the lock icon in the upper right corner to authenticate to the given directory (Figure 6-12).

Figure 6-12. *Clicking the lock icon allows authentication to the target directory.*

Just like other directories, from this point, you can create managed preferences for user, group, computer, or computer group records using the techniques shown in the rest of this book. Though we'd prefer that you keep reading straight through to the end, feel free to jump ahead to Chapter 10 and try some of the recipes.

Delivery with OpenLDAP

OpenLDAP (http://openldap.org) is an open-source LDAP implementation. In fact, it's the exact open-source component that Apple uses in Mac OS X Server's Open Directory. This means that you can take advantage of OpenLDAP, too, for delivery of Managed Preferences.

While there are some basic changes you need to make to an OpenLDAP schema in order to deliver Managed Preferences to Macintosh computers, there are too many possible configurations to go through each one, or to present a single solution that fits every need. If you're using OpenLDAP as a centralized directory service, we can only assume you are an advanced user with a good knowledge of your LDAP server setup and network environment. We can only give you pointers for getting started. If this is not the case, or updating OpenLDAP is beyond your comfort zone, check in with the person who configures this service in your organization, or hire someone with the background to assist you.

No matter your setup, though, you'll need to add the basic Apple schema additions to your OpenLDAP configuration.

Add the Apple Schema to OpenLDAP

Because Apple itself uses OpenLDAP, the schema additions that it uses are available for the taking. In the /etc/openldap/schema/ directory on any Mac OS X machine, you'll find the apple.schema and apple_auxilliary.schema files. These are the basic additions needed to add the Apple attributes to the LDAP directory. You will need to include these attributes in your LDAP offerings to be able to deploy Managed Preferences.

From a Mac OS X machine, copy /etc/openldap/schema/apple.schema to the schema directory on your OpenLDAP server. This is typically /etc/ldap/schema, but it may be different in your configuration.

Consider Indexing

In a small or test environment, you may not ever notice the lookup patterns that Mac OS X uses, as LDAP lookups can still be relatively fast, even with data that are not indexed. However, in a larger environment with hundreds of user and group records, LDAP lookups can become noticeably slow for Mac OS X clients if the attributes that it looks up are not indexed. At the very least, you must ensure that uid, uidNumber, apple-generateduid, and—for groups—apple-group-memberguid are indexed in LDAP.

Bind Mac OS X to OpenLDAP

Once OpenLDAP is configured properly, you can treat it like any directory. You'll need to bind your Mac OS X client machines to the server. Start by opening Directory Utility.app from /System/Library/CoreServices (or /Applications/Utilities under 10.5).

1. Open Directory Utility.app. Click the lock icon in the lower left-hand corner to authenticate, if necessary. Double-click the entry for the LDAP service (Figure 6-13).

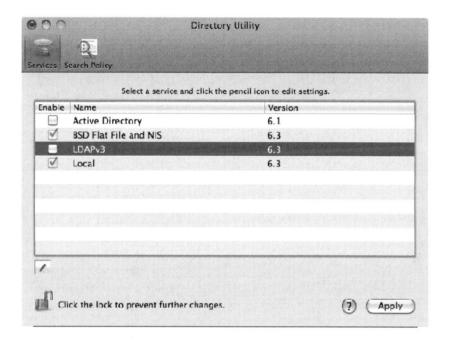

Figure 6-13. *Directory Utility showing available directory services.*

2. You'll be presented with a dialog box that asks for the server's name or IP address (Figure 6-14). Enter the fully-qualified domain name or IP address in the box. Once entered, the dialog expands to verify the LDAP mappings you wish to use. Ensure that the "Pick a Template" menu displays "RFC 2307 (Unix)." You should also double-check that the LDAP search base meets your needs. Click the "Continue" button.

NOTE: When using an OpenLDAP server, even though the schema extensions for Managed Preferences have been added, it doesn't quite make it an "Open Directory" server. The RFC 2307 mapping still have the best match to the standard LDAP attributes, although it has no concept of the extensions we're adding. We address this via the bindings on the client; specifically starting in step 4.

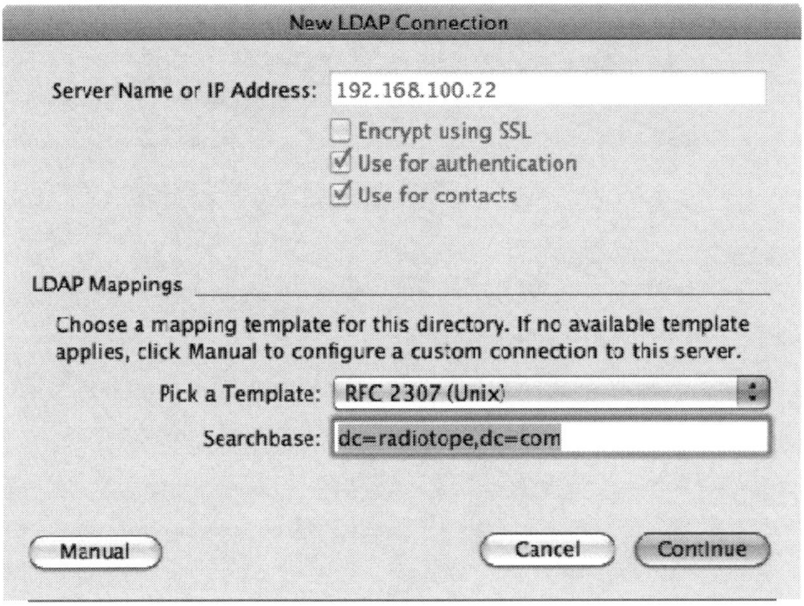

New LDAP Connection

Server Name or IP Address:　192.168.100.22

☐ Encrypt using SSL
☑ Use for authentication
☑ Use for contacts

LDAP Mappings

Choose a mapping template for this directory. If no available template applies, click Manual to configure a custom connection to this server.

Pick a Template:　RFC 2307 (Unix)　⬍

Searchbase:　dc=radiotope,dc=com

Manual　　　　　　　Cancel　　Continue

Figure 6-14. *Configuring an LDAP connection.*

3. Once you click "Continue," you'll be given the chance to name the LDAP configuration. In this example, we've called it "openldap" (Figure 6-15).

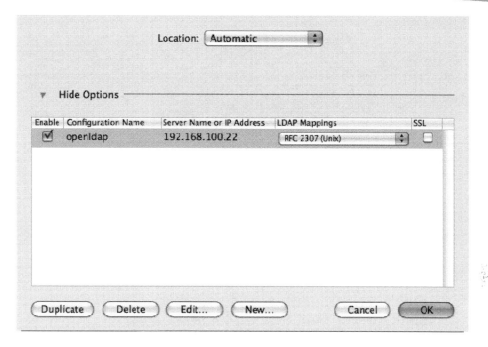

Figure 6-15. *A directory binding as shown in Directory Utility.app.*

4. In the drop-down menu under the "LDAP Mappings" column, you can now change the type to "Custom" (Figure 6-16). This will open a dialog box that gives you more detail on the LDAP mappings being used, and allow us to make the mapping aware of the extensions to the schema that support Managed Preferences.

REMEMBER: We're using the base RFC2307 mapping to match the standard OpenLDAP schema, but then extending it to understand the extensions we've added for Managed Preferences.

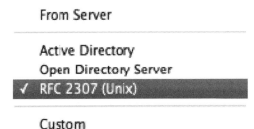

Figure 6-16. *LDAP mapping template choices.*

5. After choosing a custom mapping, you should verify that the mappings meet the needs of your environment. One typically important change is to verify that the search base for Users and Groups matches your OpenLDAP configuration. In this example, we've set the search base for users to "ou=people,dc=radiotope,dc=com" in the text field and set the scope to the "first level only" via the radio buttons for "Search in:" (Figure 6-17). Click OK when you're finished making changes, and you'll be returned to the Directory Utility main screen.

> **NOTE:** We're recommending that the search base be set as specifically as possible for performance reasons (in the example in step 5, we use the ou of "people". However, it's entirely possible to start the search from the top of the tree and descend through all branches in search of a specific record.

> **NOTE:** We've mentioned configuration of Users and Groups here, but you'll likely need to adjust the mapping for Mounts if you're using automounter. Since there are several different standards for doing this, you'll need to coordinate this setup with your LDAP admin.

Figure 6-17. *LDAP Search and Mappings customization.*

6. Clicking on the Security tab reveals some common options when binding to an LDAP directory. Take note of the options listed here, as it's likely they'll need to be adjusted to match your environment.

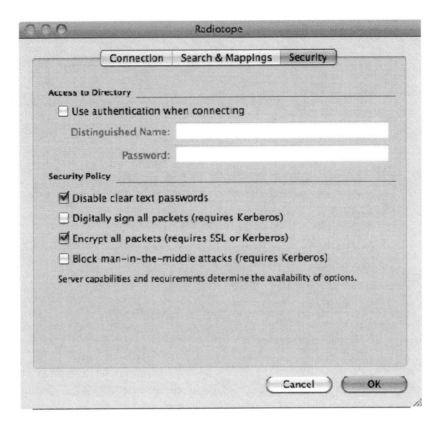

Figure 6-18. *Security options used for LDAP bindings.*

7. If you're using OpenLDAP for authentication (and not just delivering Managed Preferences), you'll need to make sure the new entry will be consulted. Click the "Search Policy" tab on the Directory Utility. Under the Authentication tab, the entry you just created should be listed by default, as shown in Figure 6-19.

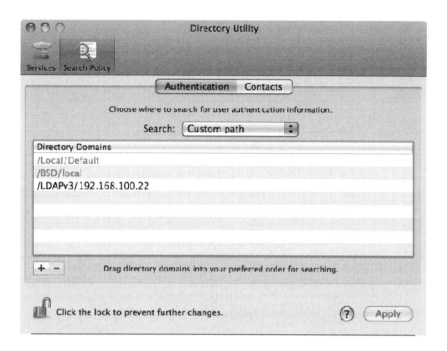

Figure 6-19. *Authentication search path shown graphically in Directory Utility.app.*

Further OpenLDAP Considerations

You may or may not be using a centralized directory for authentication purposes. In a multiple-directory environment—Active Directory and OpenLDAP, for example—only one directory service will handle authentication. In this case, you have several choices:

- Use one directory solely for delivering Managed Preferences.
- Extend the LDAP schema for Managed Preferences on whichever directory provides authentication.
- Don't extend any schema and use the local directory.

Your choice depends entirely on your environment and comfort level with the options. Sometimes, the best advice is, "don't use it just because you have it." If OpenLDAP is a secondary directory service in your environment, you may not have to force it into the role of providing Managed Preferences or interacting with your Mac population at all.

The option to use one directory applies to a scenario where the schema of the directory used for authentication can't be extended (for technical or political reasons). In this case, the main directory could be augmented with an OpenLDAP server whose only job is to deliver Managed Preferences.

The second option is exactly what is described earlier in this chapter; use your main directory to deliver Managed Preferences, ignoring any other directory services in the environment. This works well for OpenLDAP and also for Active Directory when the schema can be extended.

Of the three options listed, though, the final one—use the local directory—just may be the most compelling. This allows an administrator to keep OpenLDAP unmodified for the purposes of Managed Preferences. The next section describes this technique and the next chapter focuses solely on using the local directory to deliver Managed Preferences.

Delivery Without a Centralized Directory

It's easy to deliver Managed Preferences to all your managed machines if they are connected to an Apple Open Directory server, either as the sole directory service, or as part of a "dual directory" configuration, where your managed computers are connected to an Open Directory server in addition to another directory. If you don't have an Open Directory server, it's also possible, as we've seen, to modify Active Directory or third-party LDAP implementations to contain Managed Preferences data.

But what can you do if the following is true?

- You don't have an Apple Open Directory server.

- You don't have a central directory service.

- You have a central directory you can't or don't want to modify to contain Managed Preferences data.

Are you out of luck? No. You can still deliver Managed Preferences data to the local directory service. If you look back to Chapter 3, you'll remember that we discussed the local directory service and the directory service search path. Figure 6-20 might serve as a reminder.

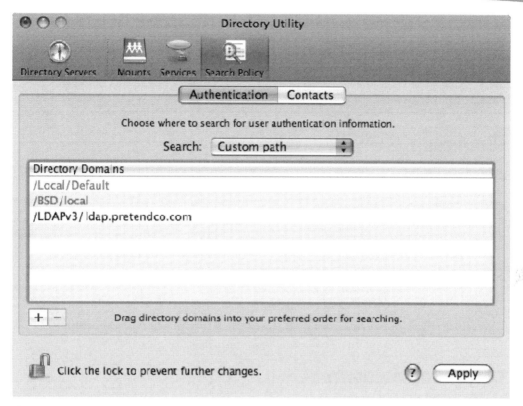

Figure 6-20. *Directory authentication search path*

Looking at the search order, we're reminded that OS X looks in the local directory first, in addition to the network directory, here named /LDAPv3/ldap.pretendco.com.

We can take advantage of this arrangement and insert our Managed Preferences data into the local directory service. Regardless of whether we have a network directory, the Managed Preferences data will be available to the local machine. This approach is often referred to as "Local MCX," the topic of our next chapter.

Help! I Can't Use MCX at All

Well, this is a book on managing Macs *with* Managed Preferences (MCX). However, there may be some scenarios where you can't, or don't want to use MCX-proper for one reason or another. Fortunately, you're not entirely out of luck for fleet management. We've mentioned some third-party products, like Puppet, and Casper that take on the role of managing a fleet of Macintosh machines. Those products provide one possible option. There is one other option, though, that we think you should consider.

In the previous two chapters of this book, we've introduced plist files and the tools that allow one to manipulate them. It's certainly possible to simply use `defaults write` in a script on a Mac to simulate delivery of MCX. Mac OS X's launchd system could be used to trigger scripts for this purpose based on different criteria (like time, or a change in a file). While a management system like this is beyond the scope of this book, we could at least point you in the right direction.

Summary

We covered a lot of ground in this chapter. You learned that since managed preferences reside in a directory, computers must be bound to the directory where you're hosting the preferences. In addition, any non-Apple directory services such as the two noted in this chapter, Microsoft's Active Directory and OpenLDAP, must be configured specifically to hold managed preferences. From then on, though, you can use all of the familiar tools to create and manipulate managed preferences.

Finally, we introduced you working without a centralized directory service, just to get your feet wet. This technique is pretty recent in the scope of Mac OS X's life and can be incredibly flexible. In the next chapter, we will delve deeper into it. You may even choose to use it over a centralized directory if you have other infrastructure in place to run local scripts that can work with the local directory.

Additional Resources

Your environment may be more complex than a simple single Open Directory server or straightforward Active Directory configuration. Additionally, you may need to automate binding for hundreds of machines. These topics are a little beyond the scope of this book. Never fear! There are other resources that cover these topics. One excellent resource is *Enterprise Mac Administrator's Guide*, by Charles Edge, Zack Smith, and Beau Hunter (`http://apress.com/book/view/9781430224433`).

Learning at least basic scripting skills is important to all system administrators in order to automate tasks. This and other chapters in this book provide some scripts that will get you started with specific tasks; however, you should be able to not only read these scripts, but also customize them for your specific needs. A good way to get started is bash shell scripting. One excellent resource for learning bash is "The bash Scripting Guide," provided free thanks to the Linux Documentation Project (`http://tldp.org/LDP/Bash-Beginners-Guide/html`). Since the basics of bash are common no matter which platform you're using, don't be put off by seeing "Linux" in the title; it'll be just the same under Mac OS X.

If you need greater details on the implementation of how Directory Services work in Mac OS X, *Apple Training Series: Mac OS X Directory Services v10.6: A Guide to Configuring Directory Services on Mac OS X and Mac OS X Server v10.6 Snow Leopard*, by Arek Dreyer and Ben Greisler, is a perfect guide.

## Chapter 7

Local MCX

In the previous chapter, we looked at using commonly available centralized network directories to deliver Managed Preferences data to your managed machines. But not all organizations have a centralized directory. In this chapter, we'll show how you can manage preferences for your machines without a network directory service.

Delivery Without a Centralized Directory

It's easy to deliver Managed Preferences data to all your managed machines if they are connected to an Apple Open Directory server, either as the sole directory service, or as part of a "magic triangle" or "dual directory" configuration, where your managed computers are connected to an Open Directory server in addition to another directory. If you don't have an Open Directory server, it's also possible, as we saw in the previous chapter, to modify Active Directory or third-party LDAP implementations to contain Managed Preferences data.

But what can you do if either of the following is true?

- You don't have a central directory service.

- You have a central directory you can't or don't want to modify to contain Managed Preferences data.

Are you out of luck? No. You can still deliver Managed Preferences data to the local directory service. If you look back to Chapter 3, you'll remember that we discussed the local directory service and the directory service search path. Figure 7-1 might serve as a reminder.

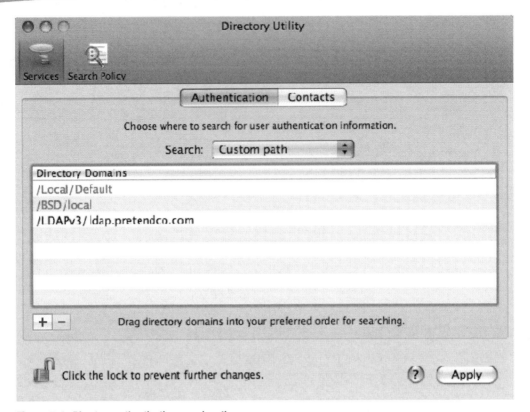

Figure 7-1. *Directory authentication search path*

Looking at the search order, we're reminded that OS X looks in the local directory first, in addition to the network directory, here named /LDAPv3/ldap.pretendco.com.

We can take advantage of this arrangement and insert our Managed Preferences data into the local directory service. Regardless of whether we have a network directory, the Managed Preferences data will be available to the local machine. This approach is often referred to as "Local MCX."

Introducing Local MCX

In Chapter 5, we used Apple's Workgroup Manager to create Managed Preferences records in the local directory service. We'll use this technique again, but this time, instead of using the local directory as a temporary workspace, we'll actually implement our managed preferences in the local directory service. We're going to outline a fairly specific strategy for using the local directory for Managed Preferences records. This does not mean that there aren't other ways to accomplish this goal, but the strategies here have worked well for many organizations.

If you have a central directory, almost certainly you have user and group information coming from that central directory. Therefore, we won't be able to manage preferences for individual users using the local directory. So our options are as follows:

- We could create groups in the local directory and add network users to the local groups. The problem with this approach is that as new network users are added and other network users are removed (because they leave your organization), you must constantly update the membership of these local groups. This option is unmaintainable in any but the smallest organizations.

- A better approach would be to instead create network groups and add these network groups to the local groups (making "nested" groups). This would allow you to leave the local group membership alone, and change the membership of the network group in a centralized place.

- You can manage preferences for a local computer object. That is, you can create a record in the local directory that refers to the local computer. We used the `dscl` command to do just that in Chapter 5. Later in this chapter, we'll use Workgroup Manager to do the same thing.

- You can also manage preferences for computer groups. You can create computer groups with a single member—the local computer—and add your Managed Preferences data to the computer groups. Preferences managed for the local computer or a computer group containing the local computer will affect all users of the machine—network users and local users—even if they are created at a later date.

The approach we will take for this chapter is to use computer groups.

At first blush, using computer groups seems like overkill. Why not just add all your managed preferences to the local computer object and be done with it?

If you need to manage only a handful of preferences, just adding them to the local computer record might be an acceptable approach. But if you have a large number of managed preferences, want to apply some to some machines, and other preferences to other machines, and want the ability to modify or test a group of preferences without affecting another group of preferences, using computer groups gives you a lot of flexibility and modularity.

By using computer groups, we can group related preferences together and mix and match them. We can create a computer group for login window preferences and apply that to all our machines. We can create another group for mobile account preferences and apply that only to laptops.

It's also possible to design this implementation so you can just deliver all the relevant Managed Preferences `.plist` files to every client, and use a client-side script to "automatically" decide which sets of preferences are relevant for the current client. This takes a lot of potential human error out of the equation. We'll look at one such implementation later in this chapter.

> **NOTE:** As it turns out, grouping managed preferences into computer groups also works pretty well for "traditional" managed preferences deployment using a network directory service.

First, we'll need to set up several things in order to use Local MCX.

Getting Started

Let's begin with the local computer record. Launch Workgroup Manager, and from the Server menu, choose "View Directories." Click the padlock icon on in the upper right portion of the Workgroup Manager window to authenticate to the local directory. Enter a local administrator username and password.

Switch to the computer accounts by clicking the icon that looks like a single screen (the third icon from the left) in the left pane. Create a new computer account by clicking the "New Computer" button in the toolbar and name it "local_computer." Your work so far should look like Figure 7-2.

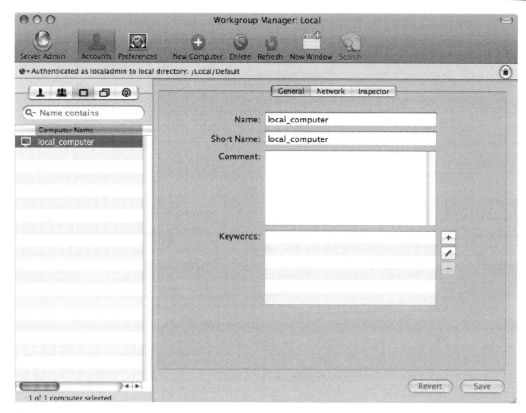

Figure 7-2. *Newly created local_computer account in local directory service*

Now click the "Network" tab in the right pane. In order for the OS to treat this computer account as the computer account for the current local machine, the "Ethernet ID" field must contain the MAC layer address of the primary Ethernet interface. We can get that from the Network preferences pane shown in Figure 7-3, which displays the primary Ethernet ID for my computer—yours will differ.

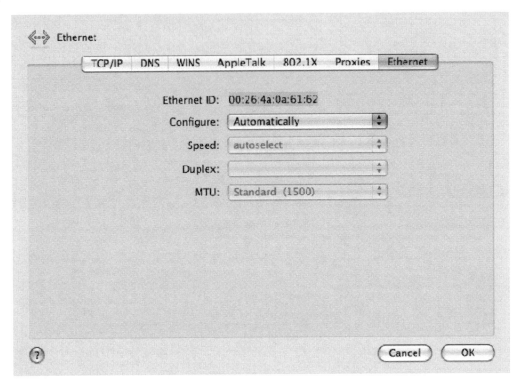

Figure 7-3. *Ethernet ID*

Another way to get this is a one-liner in the Terminal:

```
# ifconfig en0 | awk '/ether/ { print $2 }'
00:26:4a:0a:61:62
```

Once you have the Ethernet ID, copy it into the field of the same name for the local_computer account in Workgroup Manager, as in Figure 7-4. Leave the other fields in the Network pane empty, and then click the "Save" button.

> **NOTE:** Some other implementations of this concept set the IP Address for the local_computer record to 127.0.0.1, also known as the "loopback" address, which always refers to the local machine. We haven't found this to be needed, and in fact, have seen some issues with this approach. Further, in Snow Leopard, the OS creates a `localhost.plist` in the default local directory service, and this localhost record does have its IP address set to 127.0.0.1. This is a conflict waiting to happen, so we're avoiding it by leaving the 127.0.0.1 address out of the equation. This is also the same reason we're avoiding the "localhost" name, which you may also see in alternate implementations of this concept.

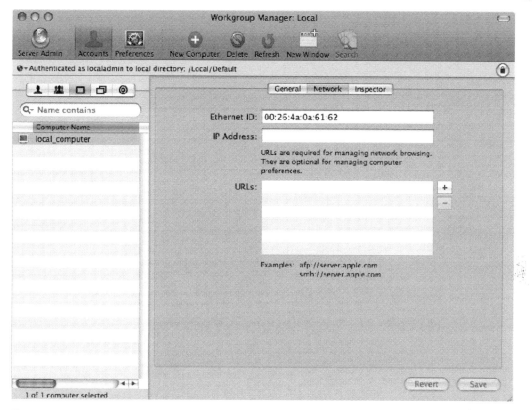

Figure 7-4. *local_computer's Ethernet ID*

Think about what we've just done for a moment. We've added the primary Ethernet ID for this specific computer to the local_computer account. We won't be able to use this account on any other computer; instead we'll need a way to create an equivalent account on each of our managed computers, each with the Ethernet ID specific to that computer. We can solve this problem, but we'll save that for a bit later.

Creating a Computer Group

Now that we have a local_computer record, we can create one or more computer groups. Let's start simply. Switch to the view of computer groups by clicking the icon that looks like two screens in the top left pane of Workgroup Manager. Click the "New Computer Group" icon in the toolbar, and name the new group "loginwindow." It should look like the example in Figure 7-5.

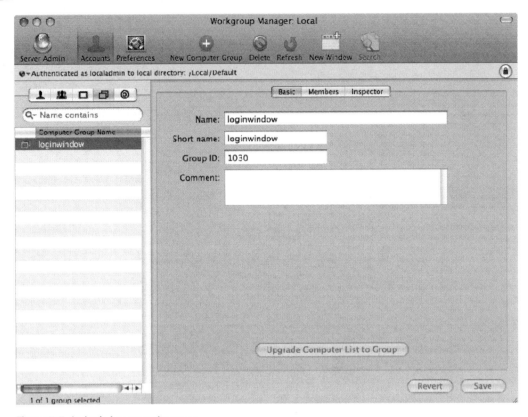

Figure 7-5. *loginwindow computer group*

Click the "Members" tab in the right pane, and click the plus button on the right. A drawer will slide out, listing the local computer accounts. Drag "local_computer" into the membership list for this computer group. Click the "Save" button. The result should resemble Figure 7-6.

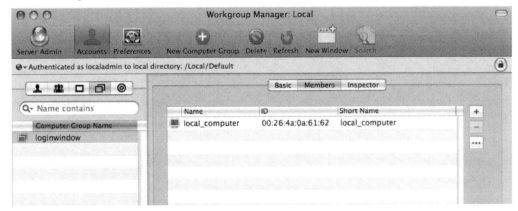

Figure 7-6. *local_computer added to loginwindow computer group*

Adding Managed Preferences

Now that the preparation work is out of the way, we can finally add some managed preferences. With the "loginwindow" computer group still selected, click the "Preferences" button in the toolbar to see the Preferences overview. Since we named this computer group "loginwindow," it shouldn't be surprising that we're going to manage some login window preferences. Click the "Login" preference group.

You'll now see a set of controls for specifying login window preferences. Leave the "Window" tab selected. In the set of radio buttons next to "Manage," click the "Always" button. Make some changes to the managed settings. In Figure 7-7, we've changed the Heading to display the serial number instead of the machine name, added a message to the Login Window, and changed the Style to show only name and password fields (instead of the default list of users).

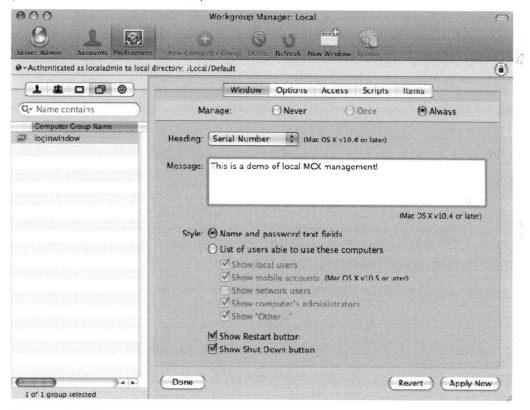

Figure 7-7. *loginwindow managed preferences*

Click the "Apply Now" button. If you log out, the login window should now reflect the changes you've made, just like in Figure 7-8.

Figure 7-8. *The login window with managed preferences applied*

If you have other groups of preferences you wish to manage, you can create additional computer groups and attach additional managed preferences to each group.

Extending the Managed Preferences to Other Machines

We now have managed preferences working in the local directory service for this particular machine. We certainly don't want to have to repeat all our work on each machine we manage—so how do we deliver these preferences to all the machines we want to manage?

As it turns out, the data for the local directory service is stored as simple .plist files. (Yes, there they are again—.plist files are everywhere in OS X!) By default, local computer accounts are in /private/var/db/dslocal/nodes/Default/computers/ and local computer groups are in /private/var/db/dslocal/nodes/Default/computergroups/. For the computer groups, we can just copy the files in /private/var/db/dslocal/nodes/Default/computergroups/ to all our machines. We can't just copy local_computer.plist from /private/var/db/dslocal/nodes/Default/computers/, however, since, as you might remember, this record has data specific to one machine.

> **NOTE:** While it's true that local directory service data is stored in .plist files in Mac OS X 10.5 and 10.6, there's no guarantee Apple will always do this. We're taking advantage of a current implementation detail, but it's one that could change in the future.

For the local_computer account, we'll have to use a different strategy. In Chapter 5, we used the dscl command to create a local_computer account. We'll do that again now, but in a script:

```
#!/bin/sh
GUID="15BEE70A-A32D-4A33-B740-93CBE95F75A4"
/usr/bin/dscl . -create /Computers/local_computer
/usr/bin/dscl . -create /Computers/local_computer RealName "Local Computer"
/usr/bin/dscl . -create /Computers/local_computer GeneratedUID $GUID
/usr/bin/dscl . -create /Computers/local_computer ENetAddress $(ifconfig en0 | awk
'/ether/ {print $2}')
```

You must run this script at least once on each machine you wish to manage in order to create a working local_computer account. You can run it more than once without problem; I actually have it set to run at each startup.

This script performs the equivalent of what we did earlier with Workgroup Manager, with one key difference. Instead of allowing the computer to create a GeneratedUID, we're populating this field with a specific value. The specific value itself doesn't matter; but it must match the GeneratedUID of the local_computer account you used when creating your computer groups and their managed preferences. This is because the GeneratedUID of the local_computer account is stored in the computer groups as part of the membership information. Look at the GroupMembers attribute here:

```
> dscl . read /ComputerGroups/loginwindow
AppleMetaNodeLocation: /Local/Default
Computers: local_computer
GeneratedUID: F4E181C7-5BFD-4572-9BBB-F659588FD74D
GroupMembers: 15BEE70A-A32D-4A33-B740-93CBE95F75A4
GroupMembership: local_computer
PrimaryGroupID: 1030
RealName: loginwindow
RecordName: loginwindow
RecordType: dsRecTypeStandard:ComputerGroups
```

The name and GeneratedUID for the local_computer account must match the GroupMembership and GroupMembers in the local computer groups for the membership to work correctly.

In case you are a bit worried that we are using the same GeneratedUID on multiple machines, don't worry. These objects will be used only in the local directory node, which is not visible to other machines—it's seen only by the local machine. Making the GeneratedUIDs consistent across all the machines you manage makes things easier on you, the administrator.

Local MCX Checklist

You'll need three things to use managed preferences in the local directory service:

- Computer group .plist files copied from /private/var/db/dslocal/ nodes/Default/computergroups/

- A script to create the local_computer account

- A way to deliver the first two items to each machine

With any luck, that last item isn't a showstopper. If you manage multiple OS X machines, you probably have a way to deliver software or at least copy files to each machine you manage. Some commercial software packages that can help you with this include the following:

- *Apple Remote Desktop*: www.apple.com/remotedesktop/

- *Casper Suite*: www.jamfsoftware.com/

- *FileWave*: www.filewave.com/

- *KACE Management Appliance*: www.kace.com/

- *Absolute Manage (formerly LANrev)*: www.lanrev.com/

There are open-source options as well: Puppet (www.puppetlabs.com/) and Radmind (http://rsug.itd.umich.edu/software/radmind/) are among the most popular. If you are an experienced UNIX hand, you can get away with nothing more than the command-line scp utility, which securely copies files to remote machines.

Advanced Local MCX

So far, we've described a basic Local MCX setup, but there are at least a few more cool tricks to consider.

Dynamic Group Membership (or "Smart Groups")

One reason to organize your managed preferences into computer groups is so that you can more easily deploy one set of managed preferences to one group of machines, and another set to another group of machines. In an education environment, for example, you may want to manage preferences for lab and/or student machines one way, and staff machines another way. Grouping your managed preferences into computer groups makes this easy.

In my environment, though, I found that I really had only two groups of preferences and two groups of machines: managed preferences I wanted to apply to desktop machines, and managed preferences I wanted to apply to laptops.

Rather than having to keep track of each type of machine and make sure the correct set of preferences was deployed, I wanted each computer to figure this sort of thing out for itself.

To do this, instead of creating a single local_computer account, I created a local_desktop account and a local_laptop account. I then added one, the other, or both accounts to each of the computer groups, depending on whether I wanted those preferences to apply to desktops, laptops, or both.

I then wrote a modified version of the script that creates the local computer accounts on each machine. This modified script determines if the machine is a laptop or desktop, and then adds the Ethernet ID to the correct computer record. Here's an example:

```
#!/bin/sh

# these GUIDs must match those referred to in the /ComputerGroups groupmembership
desktop_GUID="B4247B97-F249-4409-8EA3-BA8E168BA0DA"
laptop_GUID="15BEE70A-A32D-4A33-B740-93CBE95F75A4"

# create local computer object records
/usr/bin/dscl /Local/Default -create /Computers/local_desktop GeneratedUID $desktop_GUID
/usr/bin/dscl /Local/Default -create /Computers/local_laptop GeneratedUID $laptop_GUID

# get MAC layer address of primary Ethernet interface
macAddress=`/sbin/ifconfig en0 | /usr/bin/awk '/ether/ { print $2 }'`

# use system profiler to determine if this machine is a laptop
is_laptop=`/usr/sbin/system_profiler SPHardwareDataType | grep "Model Identifier" | grep "Book"`

# determine which record to use
if [ "$is_laptop" != "" ]; then
    computerRecord=local_laptop
    otherRecord=local_desktop
else
    computerRecord=local_desktop
    otherRecord=local_laptop
fi
```

```
# add MAC layer address to the correct computer record
/usr/bin/dscl /Local/Default -create /Computers/$computerRecord ENetAddress $macAddress
/usr/bin/dscl /Local/Default -create /Computers/$computerRecord comment "Auto-Created
Computer Acct"
# make sure the other computer record has no MAC layer address
/usr/bin/dscl /Local/Default -delete /Computers/$otherRecord ENetAddress
```

This script is similar to the one presented earlier in this chapter, but uses the output of /usr/sbin/system_profiler to determine if the machine is a desktop or a laptop. It then adds the Ethernet ID to the correct computer account (local_desktop or local_laptop), and makes sure the Ethernet ID is empty in the other account for good measure.

With this configuration, it's possible to push out all the computer groups (holding managed preferences) to all machines. But since the machine dynamically connects itself to either the local_laptop or local_desktop, only those preferences applicable to it are applied.

You might use the same ideas to automatically categorize a machine as a "staff" machine or a "student" machine. Of course, in this case, system_profiler will be of no help, but you might have some other way of telling, based on machine name or some file placed on each machine.

If you are counting on managed preferences to enforce organizational policies, then you'll also need a configuration management solution that ensures this script is in place and stays unaltered, and that all your computer group .plist files remain in place. Some candidates for this job include Radmind and Puppet.

Local MCX Issues

When you create computer records in the default local directory containing Managed Preferences data, you'll start seeing some warnings in the system log that will resemble these:

```
Mar  6 17:43:56 macbookpro com.apple.loginwindow[39]: MCXCCacheGraph(local_computer,
dsRecTypeStandard:Computers): Cannot cache because an existing record named
"local_computer" has conflicting attributes and must be deleted before caching.
```

```
Mar  6 17:43:56 macbookpro com.apple.loginwindow[39]: MCXD.getComputerInfoFromStartup:
MCXCCacheGraph() == -2 (MCXCCacheGraph(local_computer, dsRecTypeStandard:Computers):
Cannot cache because an existing record named "local_computer" has conflicting
attributes and must be deleted before caching.)
```

```
Mar  6 19:48:52 macbookpro
/System/Library/CoreServices/ManagedClient.app/Contents/MacOS/ManagedClient[92889]:
MCXCCacheGraph(local_computer, dsRecTypeStandard:Computers): Cannot cache because an
existing record named "local_computer" has conflicting attributes and must be deleted
before caching.

Mar  6 19:48:52 macbookpro
/System/Library/CoreServices/ManagedClient.app/Contents/MacOS/ManagedClient[92889]:
MCXD.getComputerInfoFromStartup: MCXCCacheGraph() == -2 (MCXCCacheGraph(local_computer,
dsRecTypeStandard:Computers): Cannot cache because an existing record named
"local_computer" has conflicting attributes and must be deleted before caching.)
```

Even with these warnings, managed preferences still work, so you can ignore them if you'd like. But there is another related issue you may see: on startup, the local_computer account might get deleted from /private/var/db/dslocal/nodes/ Default/computers/. If you have a script that creates (or recreates) this account at startup, you might not even notice that this happens, because your script recreates the account after the OS deletes it. Even if you don't have a startup script, you may not see this issue; not every organization that is using Local MCX has encountered it.

Both of these issues are triggered by the same underlying cause. In a "traditional" Managed Preferences deployment, where the Managed Preferences data comes from a network directory service, the OS creates a cache of local computer account and Managed Preferences data in the local directory service with the same name as the computer account from the network directory service. When the local directory service is also the source of the Managed Preferences data, there is already a computer record in the local directory—the same record it's trying to cache! This explains the MCXCCacheGraph errors in the log. It may also explain the disappearing local computer records, as the OS may be deleting what it thinks are stale cache files.

There is a fix for these issues, but it's up to you if it's worth the trouble.

MCX in Alternate Directory Nodes

You may remember from Chapter 3 that OS X supports connecting to multiple network directory services at the same time. What's also true, but less known, is that OS X supports multiple local directory services as well. You may have noticed that the local directory service we've used so far is located at /private/var/db/dslocal/nodes/ Default/. There's a clue in the path name—the directory named "nodes" implies support for multiple nodes, and "Default" is merely the *default* local node.

It turns out that you can create multiple local nodes within the /private/var/db/ dslocal/nodes/ directory. So what we are going to do is create a special local node just for MCX data and move our computers and computer groups into the new node. This will allow the OS to cache local computer data in the Default local node, since it will not also be the source of the MCX data. At a shell prompt, do this:

```
cd /var/db/dslocal/nodes
sudo mkdir MCX
sudo chmod 700 MCX
sudo mkdir MCX/computers
sudo mkdir MCX/computergroups
sudo mv Default/computers/* MCX/computers/
sudo mv Default/computergroups/* MCX/computergroups/
```

We create a new node named "MCX" simply by creating a new directory of that name in /private/var/db/dslocal/nodes/. We change its permissions to match the existing Default directory, and then create computer and computer groups directories under MCX. Finally, we move the existing computer and computer group .plist files from the Default node to the new MCX node.

Next, we need to make Directory Service aware of the changes we made. We could reboot, but that takes too long, so instead we just kill Directory Service—launchd will restart it for us.

```
sudo killall DirectoryService
```

Next, we need to tell Directory Service to actually use the new node. Launch the Directory Utility application. You can find it in /Applications/Utilities on Leopard, and in /System/Library/CoreServices on Snow Leopard. If you can't see the toolbar at the top of the Directory Utility window, click "Show Advanced Settings." Click the "Search Policy" icon in the toolbar. Click the padlock icon and authenticate. Make sure the "Search" pop-up is set to "Custom path." The results should be similar to those shown earlier in Figure 7-2.

Let's add our new local node to our search path. Click the plus button under the list of directory domains. A sheet should appear like the one in Figure 7-9.

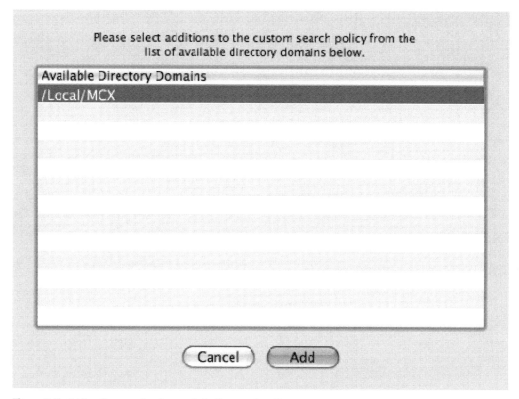

Figure 7-9. *Adding the new directory node to the search path*

Select the /Local/MCX directory domain and click the "Add" button. The new node will appear at the bottom of the search list. If you have a network directory in your list, move /Local/MCX above it, so it looks like Figure 7-10. Click the "Apply" button.

> **NOTE:** Moving the /Local/MCX directory above any network directory is probably not strictly necessary. Managed Preferences will still work if /Local/MCX is at the bottom of the search path. But for performance reasons, you'll probably want to make sure all the local nodes are searched before any network node. Searching local nodes is faster than searching a network node. Therefore, I move the new local node before any network nodes.

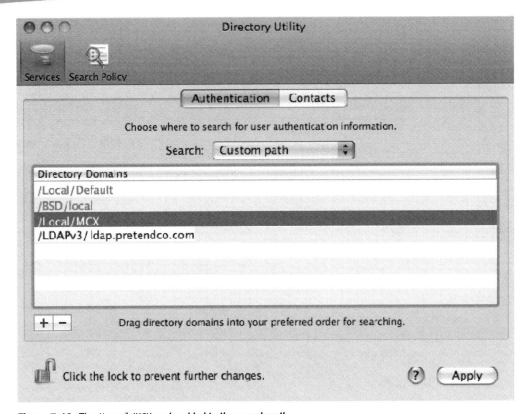

Figure 7-10. *The /Local/MCX node added to the search path*

If you now log out and back in, you'll find that all your managed preferences behave exactly as before. And they should—the managed preferences themselves haven't changed; they are just coming from a different source. But—and this is the whole point of this exercise—you'll find the MCXCCacheGraph errors are no longer being written to your system log.

If you launch Workgroup Manager and View Directories, you'll find you can view the new /Local/MCX node by clicking the global icon or text that reads "Viewing local directory: /Local/Default" in the top left of the window. A pop-up menu will appear, and you can select "Other" from the list, as shown in Figure 7-11.

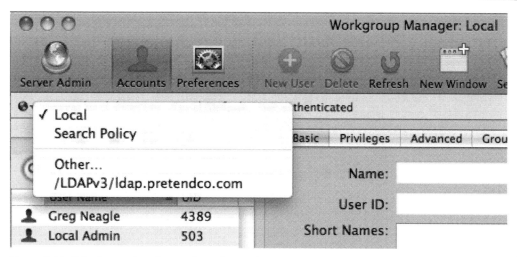

Figure 7-11. *Selecting another directory in Workgroup Manager*

After selecting "Other" from the pop-up menu, a list of available directories will appear. Under "Local," select the new "MCX" node, as shown in Figure 7-12.

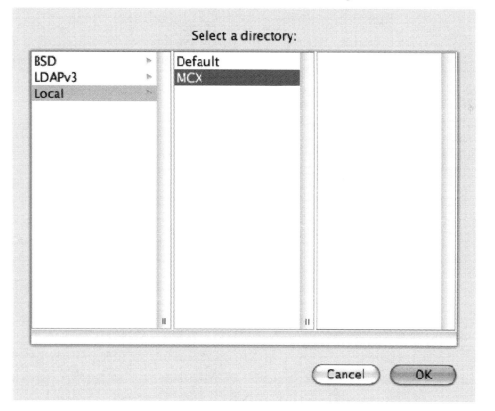

Figure 7-12. *Selecting the /Local/MCX directory*

When you choose /Local/MCX, the text will change to "Viewing local directory: /Local/MCX. Not authenticated," as in Figure 7-13.

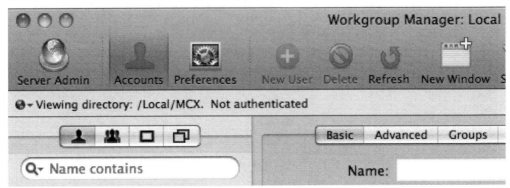

Figure 7-13. *Viewing the /Local/MCX node*

You can now *view* the computer and computer group records, but you cannot change them. If you click the padlock icon on the right side of the window to authenticate, you'll probably discover that you cannot authenticate. Ugh! Does that mean we're resigned to using the command line to edit Managed Preferences in this new /Local/MCX node?

No. You can still use Workgroup Manager; you just need to create one more record in the new /Local/MCX directory. When Workgroup Manager prompts for authentication for a directory, it's looking for an administrator from the directory you are trying to access. So we need to create a local admin account in the new /Local/MCX node. The only purpose for this account is to be able to authenticate in Workgroup Manager, so it doesn't need a home directory or working shell.

Since we can't yet use Workgroup Manager to edit records in the /Local/MCX node (this is the chicken-and-the-egg problem), we'll have to do this next step from the command line.

```
sudo dscl /Local/MCX create /Users/mcxadmin
sudo dscl /Local/MCX create /Users/mcxadmin uid 8080
sudo dscl /Local/MCX create /Users/mcxadmin gid 80
sudo dscl /Local/MCX create /Users/mcxadmin shell /usr/bin/false
sudo dscl /Local/MCX create /Users/mcxadmin home /var/empty
sudo dscl /Local/MCX passwd /Users/mcxadmin
New Password: <enter a password for the account>
```

We've created a user named "mcxadmin" in the /Local/MCX node. We assigned it an arbitrary uid of 8080 (it's best to pick one not in use by any other local account in the /Local/Default node, or any network directory service your machines may be using). By assigning it a gid of 80, we've placed it into the "admin" group in /Local/Default, which has a gid of 80. We set its shell to /usr/bin/false, which prevents anyone from using this account to log into the machine, and set the home directory to /var/empty for good measure. Finally, we set a password for the account.

Returning to Workgroup Manager, we can now use the new mcxadmin account to authenticate against the /Local/MCX node, and now we can edit directory records as well.

That was a lot of effort to get rid of a seemingly harmless warning message. If you decide to go forward with this change, you'll need to modify any scripts you have that create or modify the local computer record, since it now is in a different directory node. You'll need to modify your delivery mechanisms to deliver the computer and computer group .plist files to their new location as well, which might entail building all new packages for your software delivery system. You'll need to find a way to add the new /Local/MCX node to the Directory Service search path on all your managed machines. This can be done with dscl by manipulating the CSPSearchPath in the /Search node:

```
dscl /Search create / CSPSearchPath /Local/Default /BSD/local /Local/MCX
/LDAPv3/ldap.pretendco.com
```

You could even add this to your script that creates the local computer record.

So, yes, this is a non-trivial change (which is why it's in the "Advanced" section of this chapter). But now caching of local computer Managed Preferences data works as designed, and MCXCCacheGraph is happy.

More Local DS Node Tricks

There are some other things you can do with an alternate local directory node. One that might be useful to you is to use it for a hidden administrator account. We already created an mcxadmin account in the /Local/MCX node, but we set it up so it's not usable as a login account. You could decide to make it a full-blown login account by giving it a home directory and a valid shell:

```
sudo mkdir /var/mcxadmin
sudo chown mcxadmin /var/mcxadmin
sudo dscl /Local/MCX create /Users/mcxadmin home /var/mcxadmin
sudo dscl /Local/MCX create /Users/mcxadmin shell /bin/bash
```

You should now be able to log in as "mcxadmin." But this account will not show up in the Accounts preferences pane, or in the login window list. Since we've created the home directory under /var, it doesn't show up under /Users. It is hidden from all but the cleverest users. (Like ones who have read this book!) One more benefit—users cannot boot off an OS X install CD and reset the password for this account.

Summary

This chapter covers some pretty advanced topics. The Local MCX approach is a powerful and useful way to manage preferences if you cannot use a central directory service. But it requires some knowledge of scripting, and absolutely relies on some method to distribute files or software packages to each client.

Using Local MCX is also a great way to experiment with various Managed Preferences configurations without worrying about affecting a bunch of machines in your organization. You can test a configuration on a single machine, and only when you are happy with it, replicate it to other machines.

## Chapter 8

Compositing Preferences

In previous chapters, we've mentioned that you can manage preferences for users, groups, computers, and computer groups. But what happens if a given preference is managed for multiple objects? For example, let's say you manage the Dock settings for the "MyOrgUsers" group, which contains all the users in your organization, and also manage the Dock settings for "Joe User," a specific user in your organization, who also happens to be a member of "MyOrgUsers."

In this chapter, we'll be looking at the answers to questions like this. We'll examine how managed preferences are combined, or "composited," and how preferences set at one level may override those set at another level. We'll also make some recommendations for organizing your managed preferences to make it easy to apply policy to most of the machines in your organization, while still having the flexibility to handle exceptions to that policy.

Managed Preference Interactions

There are three types of managed preference interactions you should be aware of:

- *Inheritance*: Groups can contain users and other groups. Computer groups can contain computers and other computer groups. So preferences managed for a parent group or computer group are inherited by the children of that group. If Joe User is a member of the MyOrgUsers group, preferences set for MyOrgUsers will be inherited by Joe.

- *Combined*: Some sets of managed preferences can be combined. These mostly involve lists of items. For example, you specify that members of the group MyOrgUsers should have an icon for Firefox in their Docks, and you also specify that Joe User should have an icon for Thunderbird in his Dock. Joe will have both Firefox and Thunderbird in his Dock because these preferences have been combined from the MyOrgUsers group and the user record for Joe User.

- *Override:* Most managed preferences don't lend themselves to combining because they are a single value rather than a list, and instead will override the same preference set at another level. If you had set the Dock for MyOrgUsers to autohide, but set the Dock for Joe User to not autohide, the user-level setting overrides the group-level setting, and, so, for Joe, his Dock would not autohide.

Preferences Precedence

The managed preference interactions of "Inheritance" and "Combined" are fairly easy to understand. A user inherits managed preferences from all the objects the user or the user's computer is a member of—groups of users, computer groups, and the specific user and computer objects that correspond to the user account and the computer. Managed preferences that don't conflict with one another are combined.

However, in the case where preferences set at one level conflict with preferences set at another level, it's helpful to know the order of precedence—that is, the order in which one level overrides another. Here's the order, with highest precedence on top:

- User
- Computer
- Computer Group
- Group (of users)

A preference set at the computer level would override a preference set at the group level. Preferences set for individual users have the highest precedence. This is a useful arrangement that neatly solves a common problem. Let's say your organization has decided, in the interests of security, to enforce a password-protected screen saver to activate after five minutes of inactivity. Since this policy should apply to all machines, you apply it at the computer group level, to a group that includes all the computers in your organization. Shortly after your implementation, an executive vice president calls tech support to complain about this screen saver. After heated discussion, it is decided to relax the policy for this user only. You could then set a more relaxed screen saver policy at the user level for the vice president. Since user-level managed preferences have precedence over computer group–level managed preferences, the vice president gets what he wants.

This precedence of managed preferences suggests a strategy to use when implementing your managed preferences. Preferences that should apply to all users in your organization might be best applied at the computer group level. These managed preferences will take effect for all users of a given machine—even local users that do not have network directory accounts.

> **NOTE:** This is an important point to remember. Preferences managed for computers or computer groups apply to *all* users of a given machine. If you need to make sure that even newly created local users on a machine get certain settings, managing those settings at the computer or computer group level is the way to go.

Preferences that affect a certain group of users (like a department, or students vs. teachers), but not another group of users, should be applied at the group level. This is most useful when different users might log into a single machine. Students might log into a machine and find a very locked-down environment with a tightly restricted list of available applications. But a teacher could log into the same machine and have more options available to him or her.

These are not either/or, but can be used in combination. You can set the preferences that apply to everyone at the computer group level, and set preferences for groups with special needs at the group level, as long as you remember that groups have the lowest priority—that is, preferences you set for computer groups will always take precedence over similar preferences set for a group of users.

Finally, exceptions to general policies can then be applied at the computer or user level. You might disable CD/DVD burning on all your machines as a policy, and then override that policy on one specific machine by managing the preferences for its specific computer object differently.

Preferences and Group Hierarchy

Users can belong to more than one group. Computers can belong to more than one computer group. Groups can be members of other groups, and computer groups can be members of other computer groups. While powerful and flexible, this arrangement can also lead to complexity and confusion. If a computer is a member of two computer groups—one set to autohide the Dock and the other set to not autohide the Dock—it can be hard to predict which preferences the individual computer will get. (While you might be able to discern a pattern in this scenario, the rules for how these conflicts are resolved have not been documented by Apple and so may change in a future release of OS X.)

Your best strategy is to avoid this situation. Keep your group and computer group memberships simple and easy to understand. I like to create computer groups for very specific sets of managed preferences: a computer group called "LoginWindow" contains all our organization's managed login window preferences, and all computers are added to this group. I don't use hierarchical computer groups (where a computer group contains other computer groups), but if you do, keep the structure as simple as you can to prevent unintended managed preference interactions.

MCXCompositor

We've seen that it is possible to define managed preferences at a variety of levels: user, group, computer, and computer group. Further, users and computers can be members of multiple groups. So there is a lot of potential managed preferences data to sort through to determine which managed preferences actually apply to a given user. MCXCompositor is a process that runs at login (and other times as well) that does the work of sorting through all the available managed preferences and compositing them together for the current user. You do not have to worry about running this tool. Mac OS X runs it automatically as needed—generally at system startup and at each user login—but you may be interested in its results.

When MCXCompositor runs, it caches the composited preferences in /Library/Managed Preferences. This is considered an implementation detail, not to be relied on, and subject to change in the future. Still, it can be interesting and instructive to browse the contents of this directory on a managed client.

At the root level of /Library/Managed Preferences, you are likely to see several .plist files, and one or more subdirectories, each named after a user that has logged into this machine. An example is shown in Figure 8-1.

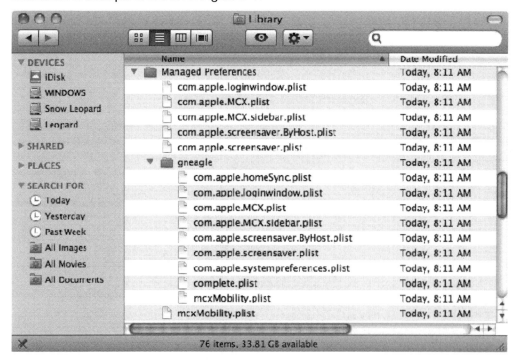

Figure 8-1. /Library/Managed Preferences

One .plist file on my machine is /Library/Managed Preferences/com.apple.
loginwindow.plist. We can examine it using the defaults command:

```
> defaults read /Library/Managed\ Preferences/com.apple.loginwindow
{
    AdminHostInfo = HostName;
    AdminMayDisableMCX = 0;
    DisableConsoleAccess = 0;
    EnableExternalAccounts = 1;
    HideAdminUsers = 0;
    HideLocalUsers = 0;
    HideMobileAccounts = 0;
    IncludeNetworkUser = 0;
    RestartDisabled = 0;
    RetriesUntilHint = 0;
    SHOWFULLNAME = 1;
    "SHOWOTHERUSERS_MANAGED" = 1;
    ShutDownDisabled = 0;
    UseComputerNameForComputerRecordName = 0;
    "com.apple.login.mcx.DisableAutoLoginClient" = 1;
    "mcx_UseLoginWindowText" = 0;
}
```

We can use dscl with –mcxread to compare this with the managed preferences I've
assigned to a computer group that my machine is a member of:

```
> dscl /Search -mcxread /ComputerGroups/loginwindow com.apple.loginwindow
Key: HideLocalUsers
State: always
Value: 0

Key: AdminHostInfo
State: always
Value: HostName

Key: SHOWFULLNAME
State: always
Value: 1

Key: SHOWOTHERUSERS_MANAGED
State: always
Value: 1

Key: HideMobileAccounts
State: always
Value: 0
```

```
Key: mcx_UseLoginWindowText
State: always
Value: 0

Key: RestartDisabled
State: always
Value: 0

Key: HideAdminUsers
State: always
Value: 0

Key: RetriesUntilHint
State: always
Value: 0

Key: EnableExternalAccounts
State: always
Value: 1

Key: AdminMayDisableMCX
State: always
Value: 0

Key: ShutDownDisabled
State: always
Value: 0

Key: com.apple.login.mcx.DisableAutoLoginClient
State: always
Value: 1

Key: DisableConsoleAccess
State: always
Value: 0

Key: IncludeNetworkUser
State: always
Value: 0

Key: UseComputerNameForComputerRecordName
State: always
Value: 0

Key: LoginwindowText
State: unset
Value:
```

We can see it's a good match. So we can surmise that the current managed preferences are being cached in the /Library/Managed Preferences directory.

The subdirectories in /Library/Managed Preferences that are named after users hold cached preferences for individual users. Let's look in mine, at /Library/Managed Preferences/gneagle:

```
> ls /Library/Managed\ Preferences/gneagle/
.GlobalPreferences.plist        com.apple.screensaver.ByHost.plist
com.apple.MCX.plist                 com.apple.screensaver.plist
com.apple.MCX.sidebar.plist         com.apple.systempreferences.plist
com.apple.dock.plist                complete.plist
com.apple.homeSync.plist            mcxMobility.plist
com.apple.loginwindow.plist
```

Most of the .plist files correspond to various preference domains we are managing, but there's one specific .plist file of interest—the one named complete.plist. Let's use defaults to examine it:

```
> defaults read /Library/Managed\ Preferences/gneagle/complete
{
    ".GlobalPreferences" =    {
        MultipleSessionEnabled =        {
            mcxdomain = always;
            source =            (
                "mcx_computergroup_loginwindow_0"
            );
            value = 0;
        };
        "com.apple.autologout.AutoLogOutDelay" =        {
            mcxdomain = always;
            source =            (
                "mcx_computergroup_loginwindow_0"
            );
            value = 0;
        };
    };
    "com.apple.MCX" =     {
        DisableGuestAccount =         {
            mcxdomain = always;
            source =            (
                "mcx_computergroup_loginwindow_0"
            );
            value = 1;
        };
        "cachedaccounts.WarnOnCreate.allowNever" =        {
            mcxdomain = always;
            source =            (
                "mcx_computergroup_mobileaccounts-laptops_0"
            );
            value = 1;
        };
```

```
"cachedaccounts.create.encrypt" =          {
    mcxdomain = always;
    source =              (
        "mcx_computergroup_mobileaccounts-laptops_0"
    );
    value = 1;
};
"cachedaccounts.create.encrypt.requireMasterPassword" =          {
    mcxdomain = always;
    source =              (
        "mcx_computergroup_mobileaccounts-laptops_0"
    );
    value = 0;
};
```

In my case, the output actually goes on for 793 lines, so I won't show the whole thing here. But if you examine it, you'll see it is a "complete" composite of all the managed preferences for that particular user.

> **NOTE:** We'll talk more about managing preferences "always," "often," and "once" in Chapter 9, but if you pay close attention to the contents of /Library/Managed Preferences, you might notice that apart from complete.plist, the other .plist files seem to correspond only with those preference domains for which you are managing "always." Where are the "often" and "once" preferences? The answer is that these preferences are written directly to the user's home folder in Library/Preferences, either as a one-time event ("once") or at each login if the preference is managed "often."

Feel free to look and learn, but you generally don't want to directly modify anything in the /Library/Managed Preferences folder. Again, while it's interesting to poke around in this folder and see what is being cached, Apple does not want you to rely on its contents.

> **NOTE:** One troubleshooting technique that makes use of this location: sometimes when managed preferences don't behave as you'd expect, you'd like to wipe things clean and start with an empty slate. We discuss some tools you can use in Chapter 13, but a brute force approach that sometimes works is to delete the entire /Library/Managed Preferences folder and restart. This clears out any managed preferences that are stored in /Library/Managed Preferences and forces the OS to re-read the managed preferences from the directory service.

Viewing Composited MCX Data with mcxquery

Rather than reading the contents of /Library/Managed Preferences/ and
/Library/Managed Preferences/username/, there are two better tools you can use to
query the results of an MCXCompositor operation, and, therefore, get a clearer picture
of what is currently being managed. The first, mcxquery, is run from the command-line:

```
> mcxquery -user localadmin
com.apple.dock
    MCXDockSpecialFolders    localadmin (User)         once    ( )
    persistent-apps          localadmin (User)         once    ( { "mcx_typehint" = 1;
"tile-data" =          { "file-data" =          { "_CFURLString" =
"/Applications/Safari.app"; "_CFURLStringType" = 0; }; "file-label" = Safari; }; "tile-
type" = "file-tile"; }, { "mcx_typehint" = 1; "tile-data" =          { "file-data" =
{ "_CFURLString" = "/Applications/TextEdit.app"; "_CFURLStringType" = 0; }; "file-label"
= TextEdit; }; "tile-type" = "file-tile"; }, { "mcx_typehint" = 1; "tile-data" =
{ "file-data" =          { "_CFURLString" = "/Applications/System Preferences.app";
"_CFURLStringType" = 0; }; "file-label" = "System Preferences"; }; "tile-type" = "file-
tile"; }, { "mcx_typehint" = 1; "tile-data" =          { "file-data" =          {
"_CFURLString" = "/Applications/Utilities/Console.app"; "_CFURLStringType" = 0; };
"file-label" = Console; }; "tile-type" = "file-tile"; }, { "mcx_typehint" = 1; "tile-
data" =          { "file-data" =          { "_CFURLString" =
"/Applications/Utilities/Terminal.app"; "_CFURLStringType" = 0; }; "file-label" =
Terminal; }; "tile-type" = "file-tile"; }, { "mcx_typehint" = 1; "tile-data" =          {
"file-data" =          { "_CFURLString" = "/Applications/Utilities/radmind/Radmind
Assistant.app"; "_CFURLStringType" = 0; }; "file-label" = "Radmind Assistant"; }; "tile-
type" = "file-tile"; } )
    persistent-others        localadmin (User)         once    ( { "mcx_typehint" = 2;
"tile-data" =          { "file-data" =          { "_CFURLString" =
"/Library/FA/Applications"; "_CFURLStringType" = 0; }; "file-label" = Applications; };
"tile-type" = "directory-tile"; }, { "mcx_typehint" = 2; "tile-data" =          { "file-
data" =          { "_CFURLString" = "/var/madmin/Downloads"; "_CFURLStringType" = 0;
}; "file-label" = Downloads; }; "tile-type" = "directory-tile"; } )
    static-apps              dock (Computer Group)     always  ( )
    static-others            dock (Computer Group)     always  ( { "mcx_typehint" = 2;
"tile-data" =          { "file-data" =          { "_CFURLString" =
"/Library/FA/Applications"; "_CFURLStringType" = 0; }; "file-label" = Applications; };
"tile-type" = "directory-tile"; } )
```

The preceding text is a partial output of mcxquery for a local admin user on my machine.
This user has managed preferences for the Dock to set a certain default Dock. There are
also managed preferences for the Dock for a computer group this machine is a member
of. If you look carefully at the output of mcxquery for com.apple.dock, you'll see the
values for the MCXDockSpecialFolders, persistent-apps, and persistent-others keys are
coming from the user record for the "localadmin" user. The other keys (static-apps,
static-others) are coming from the "dock" computer group record. MCXCompositor has
composited the managed preferences from the localadmin user record and the "dock"
computer group.

As a comparison, let's look at the output from mcxquery for my username:

```
> mcxquery -user gneagle
com.apple.dock
    contents-immutable      dock (Computer Group)      always  0
    MCXDockSpecialFolders    dock (Computer Group)      always  ( )
    static-apps             dock (Computer Group)      always  ( )
    static-only             dock (Computer Group)      always  0
    static-others           dock (Computer Group)      always  ( { "mcx_typehint" = 2;
"tile-data" =      { "file-data" =        { "_CFURLString" =
"/Library/FA/Applications"; "_CFURLStringType" = 0; }; "file-label" = Applications; };
"tile-type" = "directory-tile"; } )
```

For me, all the managed preferences data is coming from the "dock" computer group; there's no managed preferences data in my user record.

Viewing Composited MCX Data with System Profiler

Managed Preferences information is also available from System Profiler. Launch System Profiler, and select "Managed Client" under "Software" in the list of contents. In the upper right pane, a list of managed preferences will be displayed. If you select one, additional details for that managed preference will appear in the lower right pane. On my machine, it looks like Figure 8-2.

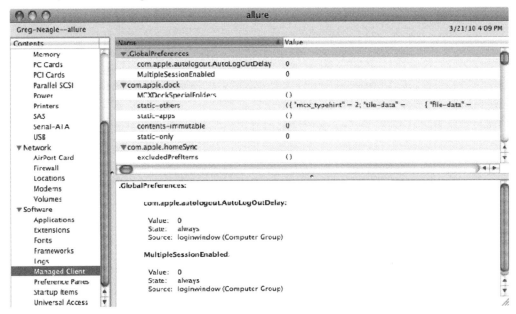

Figure 8-2. *System Profiler's Managed Client data view*

Figure 8-2 shows "Managed Client" selected on the left. In the list of managed preferences in the top right pane, ".GlobalPreferences" is selected, which causes more detail on those preferences to be displayed in the bottom right pane. In this case, we can see that "MultipleSessionEnabled" is set to 0, managed "always," and that these settings come from the computer group named "loginwindow." ("MultipleSessionEnabled" is another name for "Fast User Switching," the feature that allows multiple users to be logged in at once.)

> **NOTE:** For the command-line inclined, the system_profiler utility can also fetch this data for you. The SPManagedClientDataType will call this out specifically. Running
>
> ```
> system_profiler SPManagedClientDataType
> ```
>
> will display the same data that the System Profiler GUI does. Using system_profiler's -xml flag may be of more use to those needing to parse this output.

Either tool (mcxquery or System Profiler) can be useful in figuring out unexpected managed preferences interactions, since you can easily see the source of a given managed preference. We'll visit these tools again in Chapter 13, "Troubleshooting," as they are invaluable for this purpose.

Summary

Preferences can be managed at several different levels, and users and computers can belong to multiple groups. All of these potential sources for managed preferences must be composited together to determine the final set of managed preferences for a user and/or computer. Planning and consideration should go into your decisions about where to apply managed preferences—at the user, group, computer, or computer group level.

The strategy we recommend is to manage most preferences at the most general level possible—at the computer group or user group level. This allows you to handle special cases and exceptions by changing the preference management for the more specific level—the individual computer or user object.

You can use mcxquery or System Profiler to view the end results of the managed preferences compositing action and make sure the end result matches your intentions.

## Chapter 9

Enforcing Managed Preferences

"Enforcing managed preferences" can have two meanings. The first meaning pertains to when and how often managed preferences are applied. With Apple's tools, you can select how often managed preferences are set to the values you choose. But "enforcing managed preferences" can also refer to making sure your management settings remain in place, and are not removed or altered by a user.

In this chapter, we'll look at both meanings of the term. First, we'll explore setting how often managed preferences are enforced, or the "management frequency." We'll also consider things you can do to prevent changes to your managed preferences configuration. This is especially important if you are storing your managed preferences data in the local directory service as described in Chapters 6 and 7.

While it is almost impossible to completely prevent admin users from making changes that could affect preference management, you can implement methods to reverse these changes. Far simpler, and reasonably effective, is to avoid granting administrative privileges to users except those you trust or at least can rely on to not make your job harder, which is always good advice when managing large numbers of computer systems.

Management Frequency

In earlier chapters, we've seen some options for managing preferences with words like "Never," "Once," "Often," and "Always." These labels refer to the frequency or strength with which the preference is managed.

▪ **Never** is easy to understand, and this is the default setting for all managed preferences—it means that the preference is not managed for the current user, group, computer, or computer group object. Choose a management frequency of "Never" to allow users to control a preference themselves. Remember, though, that the same preference could be managed at a different level. Dock management might be set to "Never" for a computer group, but it could still be managed for a specific user. In Figure 9-1, using Workgroup Manager, we can see that the Dock Display preferences are not being managed, therefore the management frequency is "Never."

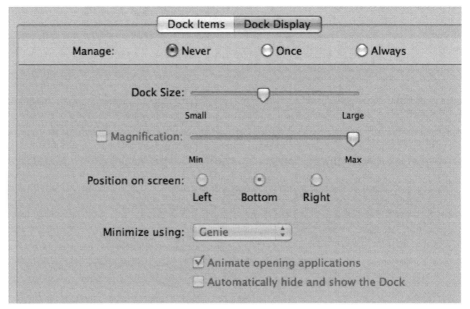

Figure 9-1. *Managing the Dock Display preferences "Never"*

▪ **Once** causes your managed preference to be applied once, and then left alone for the users to change as they see fit. This is useful to set certain default preferences for your users, but allows them to change the preferences later. Not all preferences can be managed "Once." Specifically, preferences that affect the computer as a whole instead of individual users cannot be managed "Once." Some examples of preferences that affect the computer as a whole include Energy Saver settings, Time Machine settings, and login window options.
In Figure 9-2, we're adding icons for Mail, Safari, and Preview to the user's Dock. We don't care if the user later removes these, so we set the management frequency to "Once."

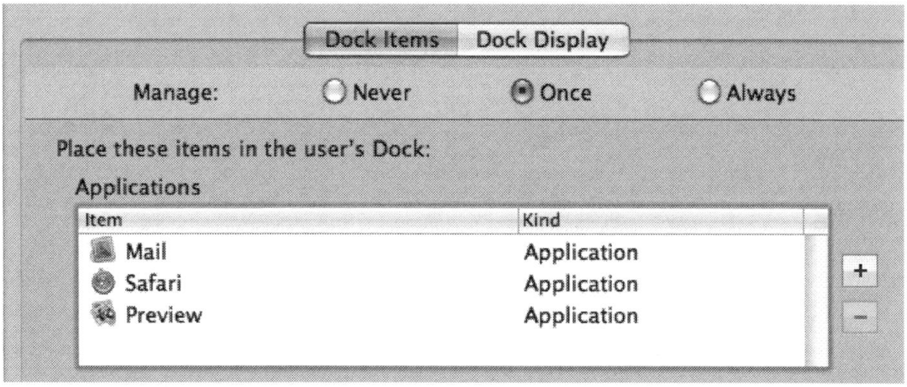

Figure 9-2. *Managing Dock items "Once"*

NOTE: Preferences managed "Once" are applied once, but if you change the value of the managed preference in the directory service, it will be applied once again. The file `com.apple.MCX.plist` in the user's `Library/Preferences` directory keeps track of when each "Once" preference was last applied; if the version in the directory service has been updated since it was last applied, it will be applied again. It's important to be aware of this; if you change a preference that is managed "Once," thinking the change will be applied only to new users, you might be surprised when it overwrites a preference already customized by existing users.

You can also use this knowledge to your advantage. If you are testing preferences that are managed "Once," you can delete the `com.apple.MCX.plist` file in the test user's `Library/Preferences` folder to cause preferences that are managed "Once" to be applied again.

- **Often** reapplies the managed preferences at each login. In Workgroup Manager, this option appears only in the Details editor. The users can change the preference, but when they log out and back in, the preference is reset to your managed setting. Apple's documentation describes this management frequency as useful for training environments, but it also can be useful for preferences that don't respond to the "Always" setting.

In Figure 9-3, we prevent Microsoft AutoUpdate from running automatically by setting it to run manually. By setting the management frequency to "Often," this preference is reapplied at each login. (Microsoft AutoUpdate does not respect the "Always" setting.)

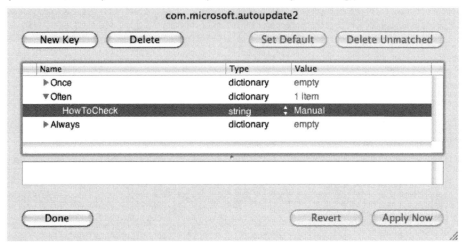

Figure 9-3. *Managing a preference "Often"*

■ **Always** sets the managed preference to your desired value and prevents the user from changing it. In some cases the user interface is updated to indicate that the preference is no longer modifiable. For example, in Figure 9-4 the "Turn Off FileVault…" button is grayed out because we are managing Mobility preferences, and have set the mobile account to require FileVault encryption. Since the users are not allowed to turn FileVault off for their mobile account's home directory, this option has been disabled in the user interface. Figure 9-5 shows the related managed preferences settings in Workgroup Manager with a management frequency of "Always."

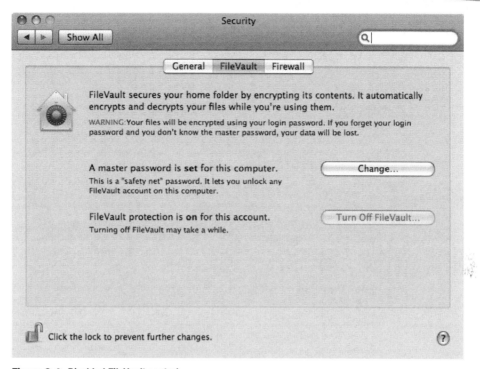

Figure 9-4. *Disabled FileVault control*

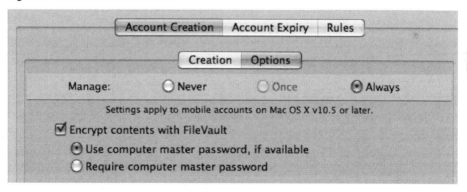

Figure 9-5. *Managing FileVault encryption "Always"*

Not all preferences respond properly to the "Always" setting. In particular, very few third-party applications support preferences managed "Always." For these, the best you can do is set the management frequency to "Often." Users will still be able to change the preference, but when they log out and back in, your managed setting will be restored. This isn't the best user experience, as users might find it perplexing or frustrating when their preference settings don't "stick." But we must work with what we have. If this is an issue for you, consider filing a bug or feature request with your software vendors, encouraging them to support preferences managed "Always."

Choosing a Management Frequency

You owe it to your users to carefully consider whether you should manage a given preference as "Never," "Once," "Often," or "Always." Ask yourself why you want to manage each preference. Here are some common reasons:

- *User experience:* You want to manage a preference to help provide your users with a better user experience: adding certain applications to their Docks so they can find them faster, disabling features that aren't useful in your organization, or configuring certain initial settings for an application for better compatibility with other users in your organization.

  For this category of managed preferences, consider managing "Once." You are trying to help your users and guide them to useful settings for your organization, but the user may have good reasons to choose different settings. You want to give the user a helpful starting point, but not force him or her to work a certain way.

  Preferences that might fall into this category include the following:

  - Default desktop picture (maybe one unique to your organization)

  - Default screen saver module (but not the timing or whether a screen saver is required)

  - Application save settings (to ensure compatibility across versions)

  - Suppressing application setup assistants, registration dialogs, and auto-updaters (because you've already performed those tasks)

  - Dock items (to help users find useful or organization-standard applications—see Figure 9-6)

  - Finder sidebar items (to help users find servers and resources)

  - Portable Home Directory HomeSync include/exclude lists

  - Default email application and web browser (to direct users to applications you can best support)

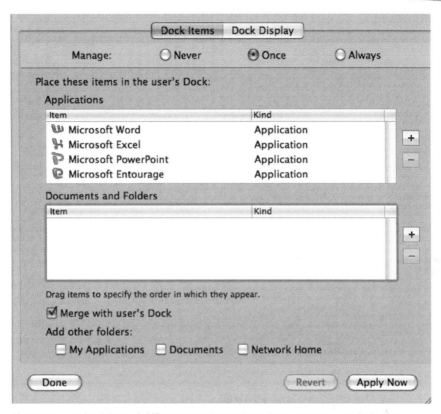

Figure 9-6. *Adding Microsoft Office apps to the user's dock so they can be easily found*

■ *Organization-specific settings:* There are some preferences you may manage because they are required to make things actually work in your organization, and, until they are configured, the user may find it difficult to do his or her job. These probably should be managed "Always" if possible, or "Often" if it's not possible to manage "Always." Some examples include the following:

- ■ Network proxy settings (see Figure 9-7)
- ■ VPN settings
- ■ Folder redirection

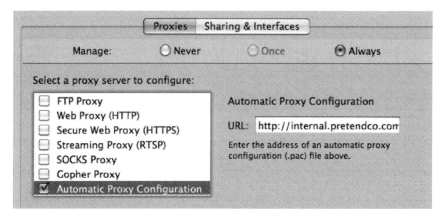

Figure 9-7. *Configuring machines to use a proxy server*

- *Company policy or security*: If you want to manage a preference to enforce a company policy or make a computer meet certain security standards, you almost certainly want to manage this preference "Always." You are protecting your organization by managing certain settings, and it's important that these settings are enforced. For applications that don't support preferences managed "Always," you'll have to settle for managing the preference "Often." Preferences that might fit into the "policy or security" category include the following:

  - FileVault

  - Screen saver activation

  - Accounts/Loginwindow settings

  - Allowed/Disallowed applications

  - Allowed/Disallowed System Preferences

  - Software Update

  - Energy Saver settings (Figure 9-8)

  - Media access

  - Bluetooth and AirPort

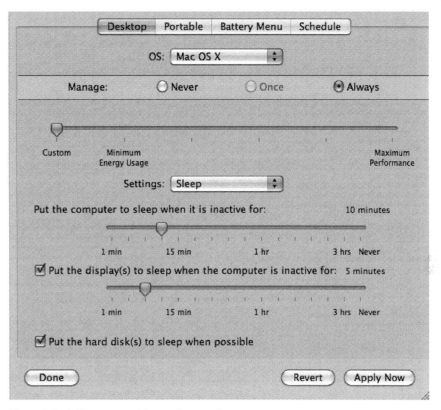

Figure 9-8. *Setting managed Energy Saver preferences*

■ *Third-party applications:* Always carefully test any managed preferences for third-party applications to ensure they actually do what you expect. As noted before, many third-party applications do not work properly with preferences managed "Always." If you find that to be the case for the application you wish to manage, that leaves "Once" and "Often" as possible choices. Consider carefully if you want to annoy or confuse the user with a preference that is managed "Often." From the user's point of view, he or she may make a change to an application preference, and later he or she may notice it has changed back. The user changes it again, and later sees that it has changed back. Unless managing this setting is very important—it enforces a company policy or security guideline, or prevents the user from running into serious trouble—consider managing the preference "Once" as a useful or appropriate default for your organization. Figure 9-9 shows the management of the document save format for Microsoft Word 2008.

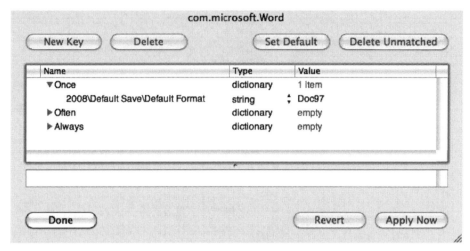

Figure 9-9. *Setting Microsoft Word 2008's default save format*

You may be tempted to manage everything "Always" or "Often." But consider that, while well-intentioned, your ideas of the "right" configuration might not be optimal for all users in your organization. Manage only what you need to, and as infrequently as you can.

Enforcing the Managed Preferences Configuration

When managed preferences data is coming from a network directory, it can be very difficult or counterproductive for users to circumvent the management of client preferences. If a user has admin rights on a local machine, the obvious way to disable preference management is to reconfigure the machine to no longer use the network directory service. Presumably, this would also keep the user from using any network resources, so the downside of doing this probably makes it unattractive to mischief-makers. However, there are more advanced methods available to administrative users that involve editing directory service mappings for LDAP directories that could effectively turn off preference management for a client.

With a "magic triangle" or "dual directory" setup, administrative users could determine which directory service is supplying managed preferences information, and remove that directory from the search path. This would maintain access to user and group information from the primary directory, so this might actually be attractive to a miscreant.

If the managed preferences data is kept in a local directory node, a user with administrative rights might be able to use Workgroup Manager to directly change or remove managed preferences settings. At the very least, a user with administrative rights could delete the local files that are the source of the managed preferences data.

So if you really, truly need to enforce certain preferences for security or company policy reasons, you need to protect your machines from having the source of managed preferences removed or altered.

> **NOTE:** Protecting the managed preferences configuration is really just a subset of the larger issue of securing the machines for which you are responsible. To truly cover all the issues and approaches to securing managed machines would require another book. Ultimately, your managed preferences configuration is only as secure as the rest of the administrator-protected data on your machines.

Protecting Your Managed Preference Configuration

The simplest way to protect your managed preferences configuration is to never give admin rights to regular users. This prevents a user from making changes to the Directory Service configuration, and from removing any local files that contain managed preferences data. This also prevents the user from doing a host of other things that are contrary to security best practices, completely separate from managed preferences. This is your first, best line of defense. This is not complete protection, as a truly malicious user might still be able to gain administrative or root access, especially on machines that are not physically secured, but it is an important first step.

Unfortunately, it is not always possible to withhold admin rights from all of your users. There are always those users who may insist on administrative rights on "their" machines, and for political or organizational reasons, you must acquiesce. Or, you may have users who, due to their job requirements, must be able to install or reconfigure software on their machines. With any luck, though, those to whom you must give admin rights can be trusted not to intentionally circumvent security measures.

That leaves the possibility of administrative users accidentally or inadvertently "breaking" managed preferences, by "playing around" with Directory Utility or Workgroup Manager, or even by deleting files from /Library/Preferences/ DirectoryService, or the local directory service store in /private/var/db/dslocal. You'll need to decide if it's worth the effort to implement a method of ensuring the configuration that delivers your managed preferences is preserved. Here are a few ideas and methods to pursue if you need this level of enforcement.

- *Systems configuration management.* The problem of maintaining a specific, consistent configuration is not unique to managed preferences. There are entire suites of software designed to help systems administrators for large numbers of machines maintain configurations. Some of the more popular:

  - *Cfengine* (`http://cfengine.org/`): Open-source. One of the earliest and most mature configuration management frameworks.

  - *Puppet* (`www.puppetlabs.com/`): Open-source. Written in Ruby, but uses its own configuration language. Has some native types for working with managed preferences data.

  - *Chef* (`http://wiki.opscode.com/display/chef/Home`): Open-source. Written in Ruby, and also uses Ruby as its configuration language. Currently, the least mature tool of the three.

These are all conceptually similar. You create a document (known as a policy, manifest, or recipe) that describes the desired configuration of a machine. The configuration engine then ensures the actual configuration matches the desired configuration.

- *Radmind* (`http://rsug.itd.umich.edu/software/radmind/`): Radmind can scan a filesystem, find changes, and (optionally) reverse those changes to a known state. If you are already using Radmind to manage your Macs, it can easily ensure your managed preferences configuration stays intact. Radmind is also a good match for managed preferences stored in the local directory service, since local directory service records are just `.plist` files.

- *Custom scripts.* In Chapters 6 and 7, in our exploration of storing managed preferences data in the local directory service, we used a script to create the needed local computer record. This script could be set to run at every startup, and extended to ensure the other resources needed were present. If you aren't using Local MCX, you could still write a script that ensured your network directory service was in the authentication search path, and made sure the applicable Directory Service configuration files in `/Library/Preferences/DirectoryService` were present and had the right contents. This is a lot of work. If you really have a hostile environment that would require this level of enforcement, we recommend implementing a configuration management solution, such as those described earlier.

Even with these additional precautions, it's still possible for a malicious user to circumvent your configuration and management systems. Our recommendation is to configure your systems and implement something to protect you from accidental or inadvertent modifications. Consider locking down access to the Directory Utility application, as that's the most likely way a curious admin user could accidently break managed preferences. (Denying access to Directory Utility.app can be done with managed preferences!) Grant admin rights to as few users as possible, and rely on human engineering to deal with the problems admin users cause.

Summary

There are four types or frequencies of preference management. Managed preferences can be applied as a one-time change. This is useful for setting certain defaults you'd like the users in your organization to have. This is known as managing a preference "Once." You can also apply a managed preference at every login, as a way to revert preferences to a known value at regular intervals. This is referred to as managing a preference "Often." Third, some preferences can be managed so they not only take a value you decide, but users are prevented from changing the preference at all. This is managing a preference "Always." Finally, choosing not to manage a preference for a given user, group, computer, or computer group is managing the preference "Never."

Once you are managing preferences, you might want to take steps to ensure that users do not (on purpose or accidentally) disable or alter preference management. This might be as simple as denying administrative rights to your users, or as complex as the implementation of a configuration management system like Puppet.

## Chapter 10

Preference Manifests and "Raw" Preferences

In Chapter 5, we introduced the use of Apple's Workgroup Manager application for creating managed preference `.plist` files. Workgroup Manager covers a lot of ground, but at its heart it is a tool for working with directory service data. There are panes for working with user accounts, user groups, computer accounts, and computer groups. Since preferences can be managed for each of these types of directory objects, Workgroup Manager also features a managed preferences editor.

The editors provided by Apple are very helpful for the preferences they cover. But what if you want to manage additional preferences beyond those covered by the Workgroup Manager Preferences overview? In this chapter, we'll explore ways to use Workgroup Manager to edit even more managed preferences. First, we'll look at using "preference manifests," which provide a useful guide to manageable preferences. Finally, we'll show you how to manage preferences for any application that stores its preferences in Apple's `.plist` format. For this, we'll import "raw" preference files.

First, let's review the editors provided by Apple in the Workgroup Manager Preferences Overview.

Preferences Overview

The Preferences Overview, shown in Figure 10-1, provides a friendly, easy-to-understand user interface for managing various preferences.

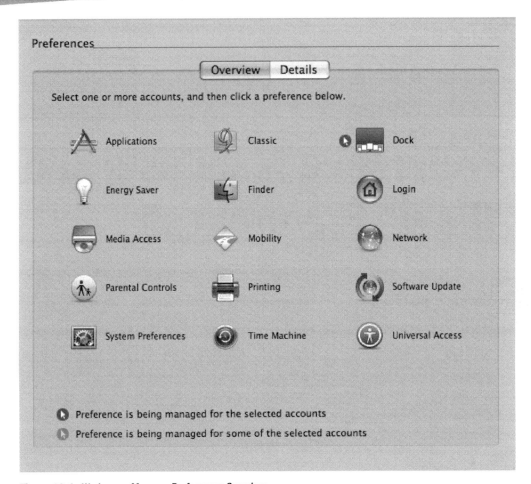

Figure 10-1. *Workgroup Manager Preferences Overview*

NOTE: You may not see every preference that is shown in Figure 10-1. If you are editing managed preferences for a user object or group of users, Energy Saver and Time Machine will not be displayed as they can be managed only for computers of computer groups.

Here, preferences are placed in logical groups. When you select a preference group, such as Login, you'll see a set of controls (i.e., editors) specifically designed for that group of preferences, as in Figure 10-2.

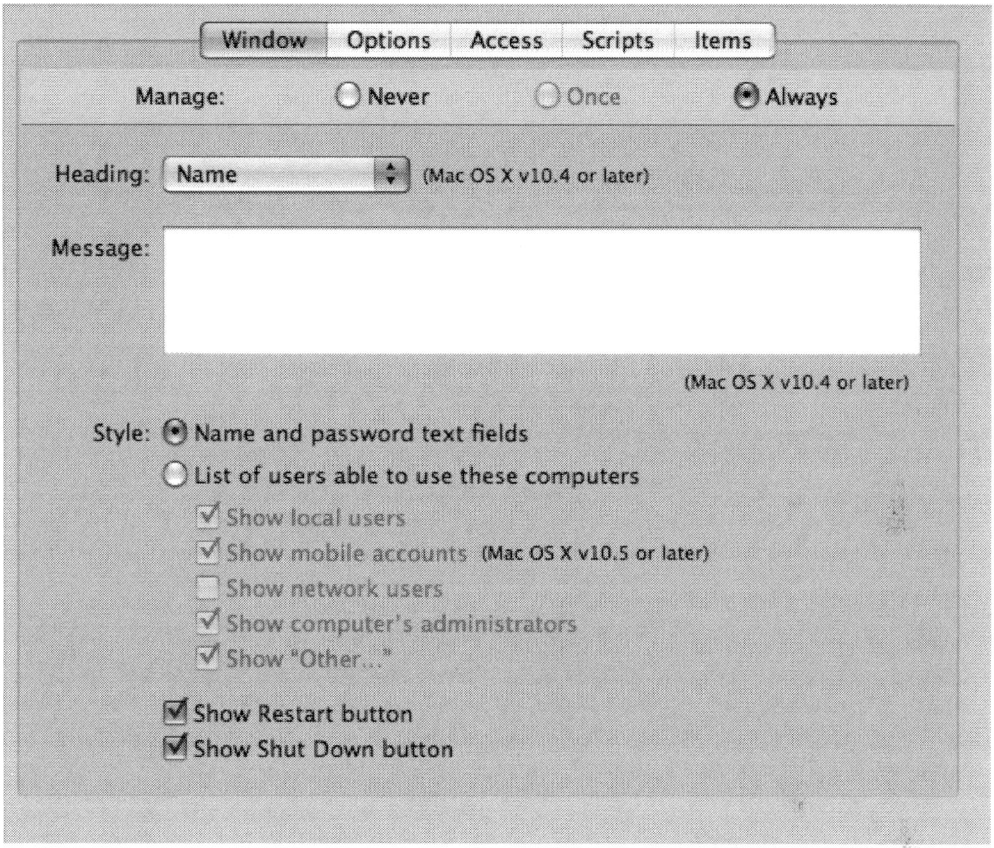

Figure 10-2. *Login managed preferences editor*

These Apple-provided managed preferences editors are a great convenience. The options are specified in language similar to the language you see in the equivalent System Preferences pane. For example, the preferences to display the login window that contains a list of users is described with similar terminology as you'd see in the Accounts pane of the System Preferences application (where the option appears as "Display login window as: List of users"). Figure 10-3 shows the System Preferences Accounts pane, so you can compare.

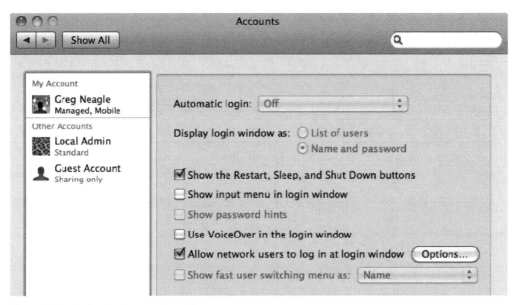

Figure 10-3. *System Preferences Accounts pane*

Apple's managed preferences editors contain pop-up menus, radio buttons, and check boxes to guide you through the available options. Apple has also provided some hints that help you understand which options are effective with which versions of Mac OS X. This is important if you are managing Macs running different major releases of Mac OS X. For example, you may have a mix of Tiger, Leopard, and Snow Leopard machines that you must support, and not all preferences apply to all versions of Mac OS X.

However, the editors available in the Preferences Overview do not cover every single preference that can be managed. You can manage additional preferences by using Workgroup Manager's Details tab in the Preferences pane, shown here in Figure 10-4.

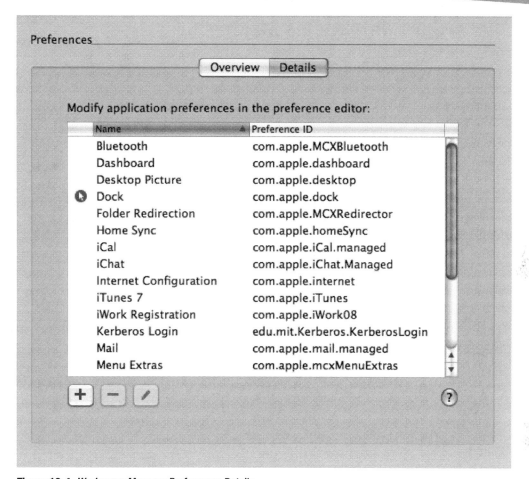

Figure 10-4. *Workgroup Manager Preferences Details*

If you look in Workgroup Manager on your Mac and don't see a list of preference domains in the Preferences Details as in Figure 10-4 (that is, the list of preference domains is empty or nearly so), don't worry. By default, this list is pretty empty. This list gets populated in two ways:

- by importing preference manifests
- by importing raw preferences

Let's explore each option in the following sections.

Importing a Preference Manifest

Apple provides a number of interesting and useful preference manifests that you can import from ManagedClient.app. A preference manifest is yet another type of .plist file, distinct from preferences themselves, which are also stored in .plist files. A preference manifest describes which manageable preference keys are available for a given application, and what type of data they must contain. In other words, a preference manifest is a sort of guide to what can be managed for a specific application.

Apple provides a nice set of manifests that you can import all in one fell swoop. In Workgroup Manager, select an item (user, group, computer, or computer group) and click the Preferences icon in the toolbar. Click the "Details" tab, and you should find yourself in the Preferences Details pane (shown in Figure 10-4). To import a set of preference manifests, click the plus button below the list, and navigate to /System/Library/CoreServices. Select the ManagedClient application and click the "Add" button, as shown in Figure 10-5.

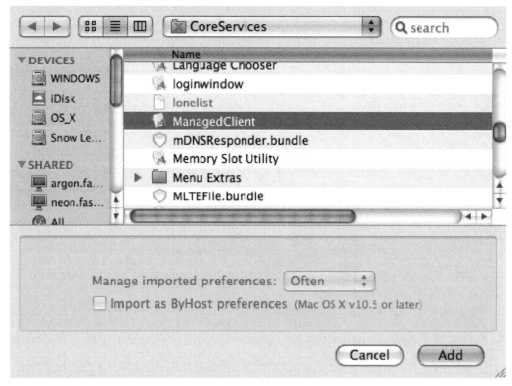

Figure 10-5. *Importing preference manifests from ManagedClient.app*

Once you've imported the preference manifests from ManagedClient.app, your list of preference domains should look a lot more like the ones shown previously in Figure 10-4.

Working with Preference Manifests

As you can see, there are now several new interesting things available to manage. As an example, let's look at Desktop Picture. Let's say we wanted to give all our users an initial desktop picture that was specific to our organization. With Workgroup Manager and our newly imported preference manifests, this is pretty easy.

Start by double-clicking the Desktop Picture entry in the list of preference names (again, as shown in Figure 10-4). You'll see a preferences details editor like the one in Figure 10-6. You may also notice that the title of the preferences details editor matches the "preference domain" you are editing—in this case, com.apple.desktop.

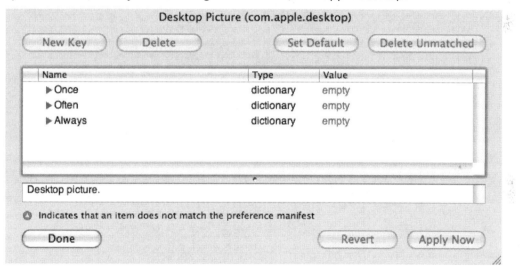

Figure 10-6. *Desktop Picture preferences details editor*

If this looks familiar, it may be because this editor greatly resembles Apple's Property List Editor application, introduced in Chapter 4. (See Figure 4-1 from that chapter for a visual comparison.) Like Property List Editor, the preferences details editor provides an outline-like structure for the preference keys you are managing. Figure 10-6 shows three empty dictionaries to start—one each for "Once," "Often," and "Always." These are three of the four preference management frequencies discussed in Chapter 9.

NOTE: The fourth—"Never"—doesn't get its own dictionary. If you want to manage a preference "Never," just don't add it to the managed preferences!

> **NOTE:** Remember, in this context, a dictionary is a collection of items, each with a name. As we saw in our introduction to property lists, dictionaries can contain other dictionaries as well as arrays or lists, and simple types like strings, numbers, and Boolean values.

For our example, we want to set the desktop picture only as an initial default, but allow our users to change it if they desire. So we'll add our managed preference to the "Once" dictionary.

Select the "Once" dictionary by clicking it, and click the disclosure triangle next to the word "Once," turning it downwards. Once you do this, the "New Key" button will become available. Click it. A new item should appear below "Once," as in Figure 10-7.

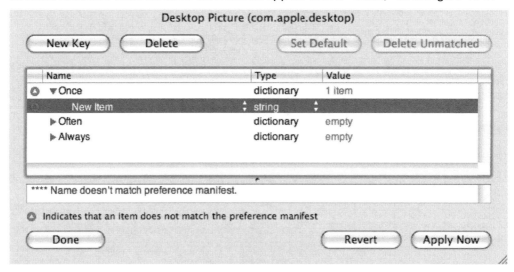

Figure 10-7. *Adding an item in the preferences details editor*

Click the name "New Item," and a pop-up menu will appear with a few choices. Select "Background." Turn down the disclosure triangle next to "Background," and a nested key named "Default Image" will appear, itself a dictionary. Click the disclosure triangle next to "Default Image," and you'll see the final nested key, named "Image Path." This key is a string, and defaults to /Library/Desktop Pictures/Aqua Blue.jpg. Double-click the path to edit it, and change it to the desktop picture of your choice.

> **NOTE:** If you have some experience at the command line, you might wonder if spaces or other special characters need to be "escaped" in path names entered in the preferences editors. They do not.

Make sure the path to your desired desktop picture is correct and points to a file that actually exists and is readable by all the users to whom you might assign this managed preference. Figure 10-8 shows one possibility (although not very interesting).

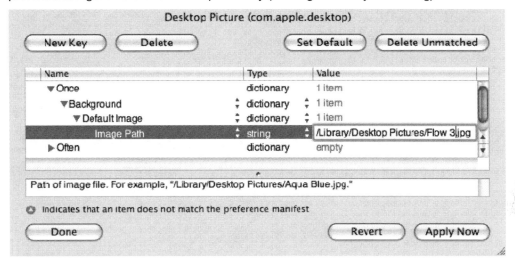

Figure 10-8. *Setting a custom desktop picture*

In Figure 10-8, you can see some of the features that make preference manifests useful. When we added a new key to the "Once" dictionary, we were shown a list of valid keys in plain English ("Background," "Default Image," and "Image Path" in this example). You can also see some descriptive text about the "Image Path" key near the bottom of the window.

Preference manifests help the administrator discover the preferences that are available to manage for a given application or preference domain and help to document their use and expected values.

Sadly, preference manifests are not common. Outside of the preference manifests you can import from ManagedClient.app, only a handful of Apple applications, including Safari and VoiceOver Utility, include preference manifests. The iLife and iWork suites are maddeningly preference manifest–free, and we are not aware of any third-party application that ships with a preference manifest, though there may be one or two out there.

NOTE: Apple has documented the preference manifest file format here: `http://developer.apple.com/mac/library/documentation/MacOSXServer/Conceptual/Preference_Manifest_Files/Preference_Manifest_Files.pdf`.

Given this information, it is possible to create a preference manifest yourself. The excellent folks at AFP548.com have provided a little more info on the process at `http://www.afp548.com/article.php?story=manifest-destiny`.

More importantly, they've also set up a repository of preference manifests created by other Mac OS X administrators called "Manifest Destiny." Here you'll find a selection of preference manifests for some Apple software not covered by the ones in ManagedClient and a few third-party applications. Hopefully, this will grow over time. You'll find the Manifest Destiny repository at `http://code.google.com/p/manifestdestiny/`.

Importing "Raw" Preferences

We mentioned early on that you can use Apple's managed preferences system to manage the preferences of any piece of software that stores its preferences in a standard Apple `.plist` file in the user's `Library/Preferences` directory. This is true even if the software is not supported in Workgroup Manager's Preferences Overview, or even if the software has no preference manifest. Those methods of editing managed preferences are helpful, but not required.

So how do you manage preferences for software that does not have an editor built into Workgroup Manager, and has no preference manifest? The answer is simple. Just configure the software the way you'd like it—typically using the application's own preferences dialogs, or via System Preferences preference panes. Then use Workgroup Manager to import the actual preference `.plist` file for the application. We'll call this "importing 'raw' preferences." This is the second way managed preferences get added to the Preferences Details view in Workgroup Manager.

Let's say we wanted to configure Apple's TextEdit application so that new documents were in plain text by default instead of the usual rich text format.

We'll start by moving the current preferences aside. Make sure TextEdit is not running, then find the file `com.apple.TextEdit.plist` in your `Library/Preferences` directory and move it to your desktop. (This is just a handy place to move it temporarily; we'll move it back later.)

> **NOTE:** Why do we start by moving aside the current preferences? It's likely that this preference file contains all sorts of preferences, and over time, many application preference files gain more and more data as they keep track of window positions, recently opened files, and all sorts of things. By moving the existing preference file out of the way, we force the application to create a new, clean file, which should make it easier to manage only the preferences we're interested in managing.

Now launch TextEdit by double-clicking its icon in the Finder and choose "Preferences..." from the TextEdit menu. Under the New Document tab, select "Plain text" as the format. Close the Preferences window and quit TextEdit. See Figure 10-9 for an illustration.

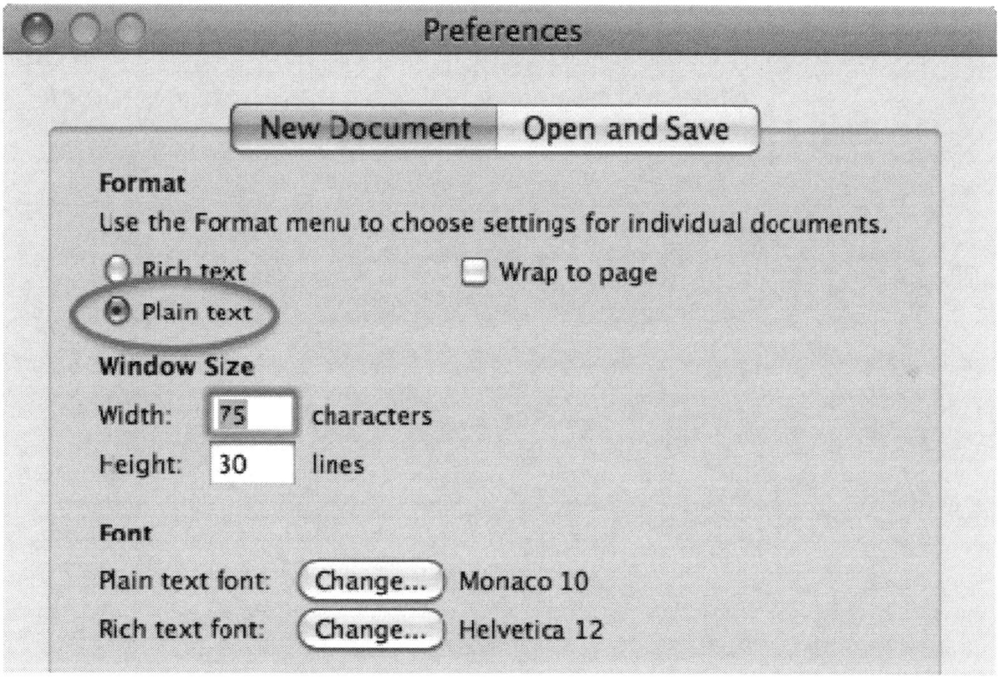

Figure 10-9. *Setting TextEdit format preferences to plain text*

In Workgroup Manager, select an object to manage (I usually just create a dummy computer group while I'm testing, and delete it later), and click the Preferences icon in the toolbar. Select Details in the Preferences editor. Click the plus button. To import the TextEdit preferences, you have two choices. The first is to navigate to and select the TextEdit application in /Applications. The second is to navigate to and choose the actual .plist file in your Library/Preferences folder. In this case it would be Library/Preferences/com.apple.TextEdit.plist. If you decide to choose the application itself, you have one additional item to be aware of, and you'll see it in Figure 10-10. You'll see a check box for "Import my preferences for this application," and it should be checked by default. Leave it checked, because that indeed is what we wish to do.

> **NOTE:** If you de-select "Import my preferences for this application," this is an indication that you'd like Workgroup Manager to import any preference manifests it can find inside the application bundle. Feel free to try this on applications you'd like to manage, but, as we've said before, very few applications ship with pre-defined preference manifests.

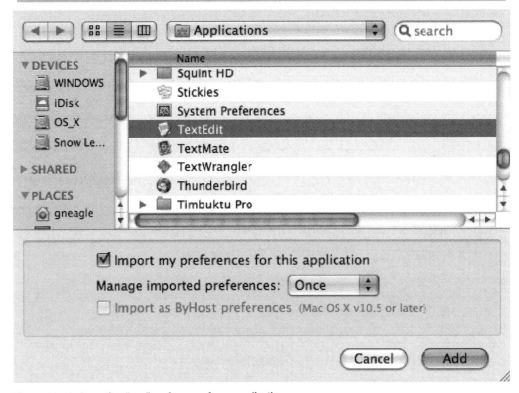

Figure 10-10. *Importing "raw" preferences for an application*

In either case—selecting the application itself, or selecting its preference `.plist` file— we want to set this as an initial default, but allow users to change it later if they want. Therefore we'll manage these imported preferences "Once."

NOTE: If you wanted to keep this setting all the time, you might be tempted to set the management to "Always," but you may find that doesn't work as expected. Few applications— and very few third-party applications—respond properly to being managed "Always." You'll have to experiment to determine if a given application can be managed "Always." For those that cannot, managing the preference "Often" is your best bet.

Ideally, the advantage of managing a preference "Always" is that the user is prevented from changing the preference's value. But applications that support managing a preference "Always" may not properly disable the related GUI controls. Don't rely on that behavior—always test.

You might have noticed a disabled option in the dialog in Figure 10-10— "Import as ByHost preferences." If you take a look in your ~/Library/Preferences/ByHost folder, you'll see preferences for a subset of the software installed on your computer. These are items that have preferences not only for each user, but for each computer that the user may use. "ByHost" preferences are designed for use with network home directories (where the user can access the same home directory from multiple computers). They allow users to have different preferences on different computers. Even if your users don't have network home directories, these preferences still exist, and may need to be managed.

If the software you want to manage supports ByHost preferences (and if it does, it will almost certainly have a existing preference file in the user's Library/Preferences/ByHost folder), you can use this option to manage those preferences as well.

Click "Add" to import the preferences into Workgroup Manager. You'll see a new com.apple.TextEdit item in the list of preference domains. Double-click it so we can examine it. If you expand the "Once" dictionary, you should see a single key named RichText, with its value set to False. Figure 10-11 shows the result.

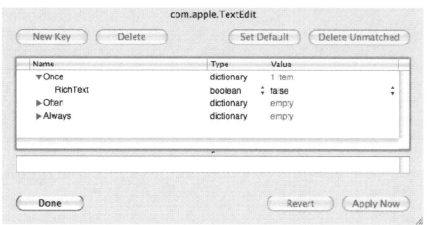

Figure 10-11. *Imported* com.apple.TextEdit *preferences*

You can now apply these managed preferences to any user, group, computer, or computer group you manage.

> **NOTE:** If you change your mind about the management frequency—for example, if you imported some preferences as "Once," but later decide it would be better to manage them "Often"—you can cut and paste entries to move them from one management frequency to another.

If you'd like, you can now move the original com.apple.TextEdit.plist file from your desktop back into your Library/Preferences folder, restoring your original preferences. (Make sure TextEdit isn't running when you do this!)

We really got lucky with this example. We started with a clean slate, opened TextEdit, made our configuration change, and quit TextEdit right away. When we imported the preferences into Workgroup Manager, we got only the single preference we wanted to manage. You will rarely be that lucky. Usually, along with the preferences you are interested in, you will also import a bunch of other preferences that just happen to be in the .plist file, but aren't among the preferences you want to manage. In that case, you'll have to examine all of the imported preferences and delete those you do not want. This can be tedious and confusing—all the more reason to give yourself a little help by starting with an empty preferences file as we did in this example.

Third-Party Applications

So far, we've limited ourselves to managing Apple software. But we've claimed that you can also manage third-party applications, as long as they store their preferences in Apple .plist files. So let's look at an example.

Many applications attempt to check for updates for themselves. For home users, or computers that are unmanaged (meaning it's up to the primary user of the computer to manage it), this can be a helpful feature. But in a managed environment, applications that check for and notify the user of available updates can be an annoyance. If the user does not have administrative rights, they can't apply the update anyway, so it's annoying to the user. And it can be annoying to the administrator as well, as they field calls from users asking why application "WhizBang" hasn't been updated to the latest and greatest.

Presumably, as an administrator, you want to control the timing and availability of updates. Updates should be tested before mass deployment, and there may be reasons that a certain update should not be deployed at this time.

So if you are managing application updates, it's helpful to configure applications to not check for updates. This saves bandwidth (so all your machines aren't individually checking over the Internet for each application's updates), and administrator time (not having to respond to each user's questions about the update notices).

Let's use VideoLAN Client as an example. VideoLAN Client (also known simply as "VLC") is a popular open-source media player that handles many audio and video formats not handled by QuickTime Player. It can check for updates on each launch. Since it stores its preferences in a .plist file, it is an excellent candidate for preference management.

If you don't already have a copy of VLC installed, go download and install one now. As of this writing, the current version is 1.0.5, and comes on a "drag-n-drop" disk image. As with our TextEdit example, it will be easier if we start with "clean" preferences. If you have an existing org.videolan.vlc.plist file in your Library/Preferences folder, move it aside temporarily by moving it to your desktop. Also move aside the VLC folder inside Library/Preferences.

Launch VLC by double-clicking its icon in the Finder. If you truly did move aside any previous VLC preferences, you should see a dialog asking if you want VLC to check for preferences automatically, as in Figure 10-12.

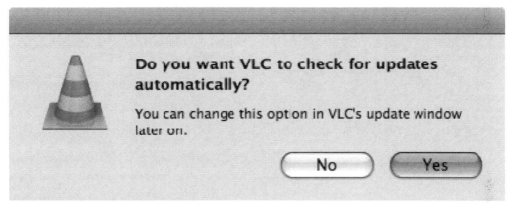

Figure 10-12. *VLC check for updates dialog*

Click the "No" button, and then quit VLC.

> **NOTE:** If you don't see the dialog in Figure 10-12, choose "Check for Update…" from the VLC menu, and then uncheck "Automatically check for updates" in the Check for Updates dialog. Quit VLC.

In Workgroup Manager, again select an object (user, group, computer, computer group) to manage, and then click the Preferences icon in the toolbar. Click the "Details" tab in the Preferences view. Click the plus button to import some preferences.

As before, we can either select the VLC application, or navigate to our Library/Preferences folder and select the org.videolan.vlc.plist file. For this example, we'll do the latter. We want to (as much as possible) enforce this setting all the time, so we'll choose "Often" as the management frequency. This will reset the managed preferences to our desired values at least at every login if not more frequently. (It's possible that "Always" would work, but it's rare for third-party applications to respect this setting, so I didn't even bother trying.) If, on the other hand, you just wanted to turn off checking for updates by default, but also wanted to let users turn it back on if they desired, you could choose a management frequency of "Once." As seen in Figure 10-13, the management frequency choices appear in a pop-up menu labeled "Managed imported preferences."

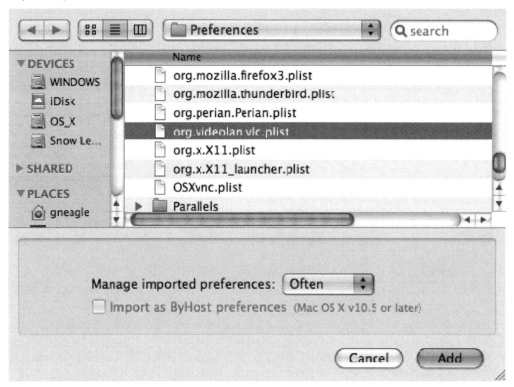

Figure 10-13. *Importing VLC preferences*

A new `org.videolan.vlc` item will appear in the list of preference domains. If you double-click it and expand the "Often" section, it should look something like Figure 10-14.

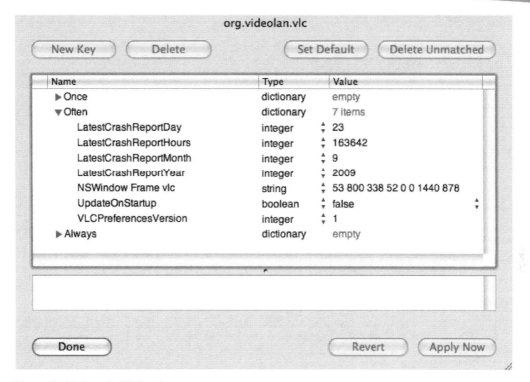

Figure 10-14. *Imported VLC preferences*

This is probably a more typical example of what you'll encounter when importing preferences from an application than the TextEdit example. You'll see that not only do we get the preference we're interested in ("UpdateOnStartup"), but also several preferences we have no interest in managing. Just select each of the preferences you don't want to manage by clicking them, and delete them by clicking the "Delete" button, or by simply pressing the Delete key on your keyboard. When you are done, you should have only the "UpdateOnStartup" preference remaining, and it should resemble Figure 10-15. Click "Apply Now" to save your changes to the managed preferences.

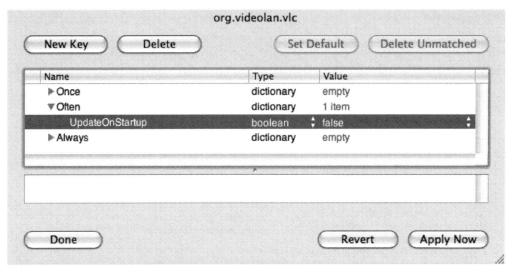

Figure 10-15. *VideoLAN Client UpdateOnStartup preferences*

As with the TextEdit example, you can now apply these managed preferences to any user, group, computer, or computer group object. It probably makes the most sense to apply these preferences to a computer group comprising all of your machines.

Summary

In this chapter, we looked at ways to use Workgroup Manager to edit managed preferences beyond those exposed in the Preferences Overview. We demonstrated importing preference manifests as a way of extending Workgroup Manager's preference editing abilities. The preference manifests included with *ManagedClient.app* add a huge number of useful manageable preferences. Finally, we discussed importing "raw" preference files as a way to manage preferences for any application that stores its preferences in Apple's .plist format.

## Chapter 11

Recipes

In this chapter, we'll present step-by-step "recipes" for accomplishing certain common preference management tasks, and briefly discuss the rationale behind managing many of these items.

We'll first look at managing the Finder sidebar, as an example of preference management used to improve the user experience by hiding items that are not relevant to your organization.

Another reason systems administrators are asked to begin managing certain computer preferences or settings is in the name of security. Organizations want to reduce the risk of sensitive or confidential information being disclosed to the wrong individuals, and also to protect the privacy of their employees. So the next set of recipes we present will demonstrate configuring the login window, the screen saver, FileVault, and more to make your managed Macs more secure.

Yet another common reason to manage preferences is to help users adhere to organizational policies. Our example here will be iTunes. You can use managed preferences to disable features of iTunes that may get your users into trouble.

In some cases, you'll be managing preferences to help your users work better as a team. The last recipe in this chapter demonstrates managing Microsoft Office 2008 to save its documents by default in the older Office 97–2004 format. You might do this to guide users toward a file format the majority of people in your organization can read and write, especially if not everyone in your organization has been updated to the latest versions of Office. Our look at managing Microsoft Office will also include turning off the Auto Updater and Setup Assistants, again, to improve the end-user experience by removing needless distractions.

Finder Sidebar

For our first recipe, we'll look at a task that falls under "user experience," where an administrator manages some preferences to help guide the users to better choices or hide items that are not relevant in the current environment.

The Finder sidebar (Figure 11-1) contains a preset list of commonly used folders, drives, and network locations that Apple feels are the most useful. However, many administrators want to be able to manage it in a way that better suits their needs. The administrator could add useful items for end-users, or remove the "Shared" section, which tends to confuse many people with its visual clutter.

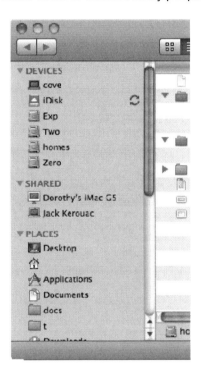

Figure 11-1. *The Finder sidebar*

The sidebar is pretty easily manually configured via preferences in the Finder itself (Figure 11-2).

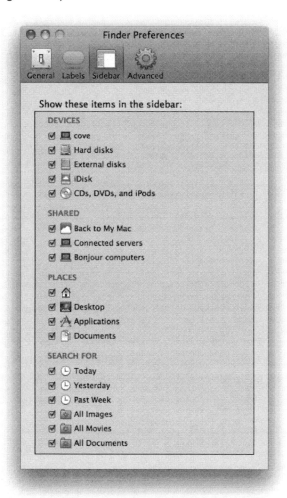

Figure 11-2. *Finder sidebar preferences*

While Workgroup Manager contains Finder preferences, it doesn't have any preconfigured way to manage the sidebar. We can add those preferences, though, by importing them into Workgroup Manager. We show you how in the next section. This way, if you want to manage these preferences for your fleet of Macintosh machines, you'll easily be able to.

Adding Preferences to Manage the Finder Sidebar

First, open Workgroup Manager, select a user, group, or computer, and then choose Preferences. This should bring you to the typical "Overview" panel (Figure 11-3). For our purposes, we need to click the "Details" tab.

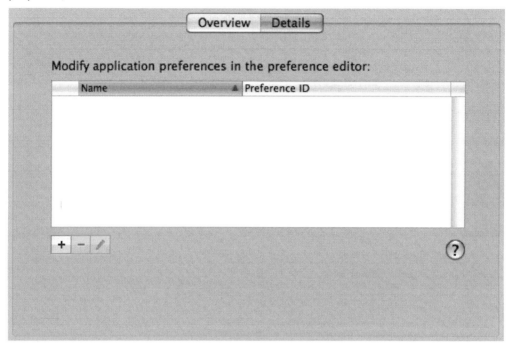

Figure 11-3. *Workgroup Manager Details tab in Preferences*

Click the "Add" button (the "+"). In the resulting file open dialog, from your home directory, choose the `Library/Preferences/com.apple.sidebarlists.plist` file and click the "Add" button.

The new preference will be displayed in the details list. From there, you should edit the imported preferences to match your needs by clicking the edit icon (the pencil, underneath the list). Importing a `.plist` file will import the preferences as set in that `.plist` file. If the `.plist` file you imported was in use by a user who had adjusted his or her sidebar preferences, you'll see this reflected in the values when you edit the list.

To remove only the "Shared" section of the sidebar, you'll want to delete the "savedsearches," "systemitems," and "useritems" keys (listed under the "Name" column). Do so by highlighting the key to delete and clicking the "Delete" button at the top of the panel, or by pressing the delete key.

Expand the "networkbrowser" key and the "CustomListProperties" beneath that. There, you'll see three values that make up the "Shared" grouping in the Finder sidebar: "com.apple.NetworkBrowser.backToMyMacEnabled," "com.apple.NetworkBrowser. bonjourEnabled," and "com.apple.NetworkBrowser.connectedEnabled" (Figure 11-4). If all three values are set to False, the entire "Shared" grouping is not displayed.

Figure 11-4. *Preferences that relate to the Finder's Shared grouping in the sidebar*

Once you've configured these preferences the way you need, click "Apply Now" and then the "Done" button. You'll likely want to copy these preferences out to be applied to other groups.

Using Workgroup Manager, click the inspector tab (the bulls-eye target) and find the user, group, or computer that you just applied this preference to. (The drop-down list defaults to Users, but you can change it to Computers or Groups as needed.)

Once the user, group, or computer is selected, the list that you're looking at will contain a record named "MCXSettings." This, unsurprisingly, contains the managed preferences that you just applied. Highlight the MCXSettings record and click the "Edit" button. You'll be shown the plain-text XML version of the preferences. From here, they can be copied and pasted into other records, on this local node or on a remote directory.

Login Window Preferences

The default appearance and behavior of the Mac OS X login window is not a good fit for an enterprise environment. By default, when you take a Mac out the box, start it up, and run through the Mac OS X Setup Assistant, automatic login is enabled for the account created in the assistant. Automatic login is rarely a desirable setting in an enterprise setting. But if you turn it off, you'll see the next undesirable default: the login window shows a list of users for the machine.

A list of users is a friendly format for the login window and is very appropriate for a home environment. It may also be appropriate in some other environments, like a primary education setting where you'd like a child to be able to simply choose his or her name (and picture) rather than having to remember and type a user ID. However, providing a list of users at the login window violates a basic security concept—given a list of valid users, all an attacker needs to guess is a password. So most organizations will want to set the login window to show the name and password text fields, requiring a potential user of the machine to know both a valid user ID and the correct password.

To enforce the "name and password fields" format for the login window, you'll use Workgroup Manager to manage login window preferences for a computer or computer group. (This preference cannot be managed for specific users or groups of users for obvious reasons.) In the Preferences view, select the Login preferences. You'll see a set of controls like those in Figure 11-5.

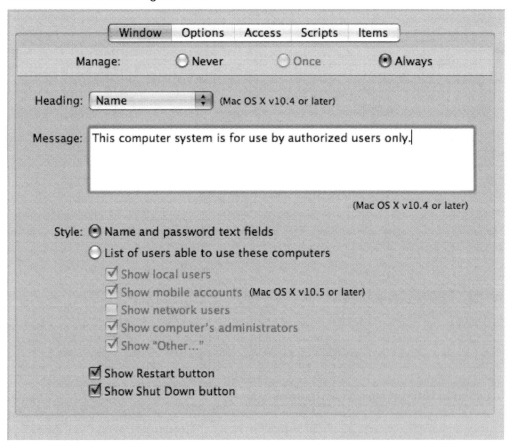

Figure 11-5. *Login preferences*

Set the management to "Always." Under "Style," you'll see the choice "Name and password text fields." That's the one you want. While we're on this panel, note the "Message" field. It's a common requirement in enterprise environments for computers to display a "pre-login" message. Here's your place to specify that message if needed.

> **NOTE:** If you need to discourage users from restarting or shutting down machines while at the login window, you'll see there are options for that in this panel as well.

We still need to turn off automatic login. To do so, select the "Options" tab near the top of the pane. See Figure 11-6 for the result.

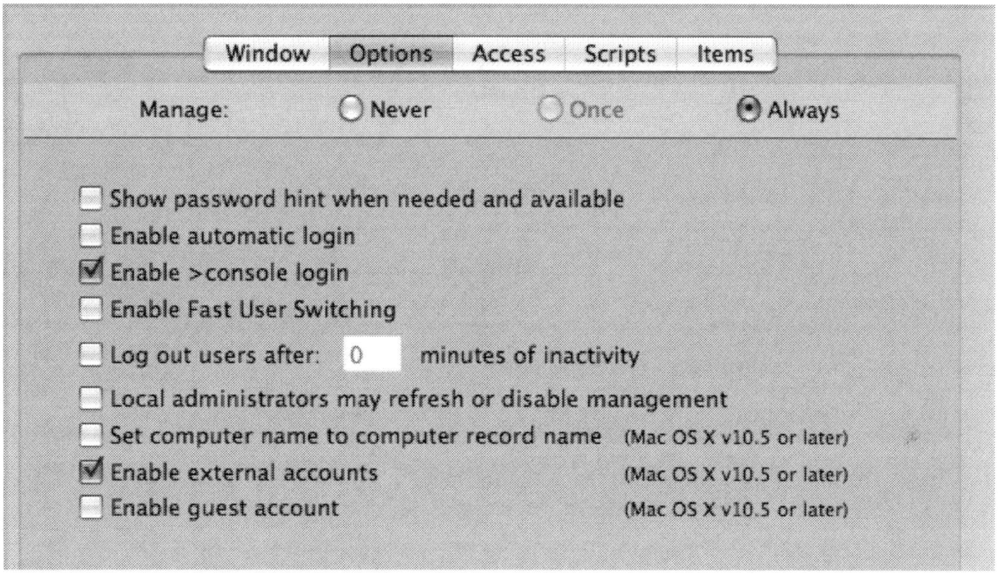

Figure 11-6. *Login options*

Make sure you set the management to "Always," and then uncheck "Enable automatic login." While you're here, take a moment to look at the other options and see if they might be useful for your organization. "Show password hint" is not recommended for security reasons; neither is "Enable guest account," but your situation may require them.

The other three tabs in the Login preferences don't control the look or behavior of the login window, but are related to actions that happen at or immediately after login. The controls in the "Access" tab can help you control which network users can log into a computer or group of computers. The "Scripts" tab allows you specify a script to run at login or logout, and the controls under the "Items" tab allow you to specify Login Items—the same type of items a user can specify in the Accounts pane in System Preferences, or by control-clicking an item in the Dock and choosing "Open at Login." Unlike the other login-related preferences, Login Items can be managed for users and groups as well as computers and computer groups.

Managing Bluetooth

If you have a need to turn off Bluetooth in your organization to prevent unauthorized sharing of data over Bluetooth, Apple's Managed Preferences can help you.

Bluetooth can be managed only at the computer or computer group level, not for users and groups. You'll find the relevant settings under the Network preferences overview. Select the "Sharing & Interfaces" tab, set the management state to "Always," and check "Disable Bluetooth," as shown in Figure 11-7.

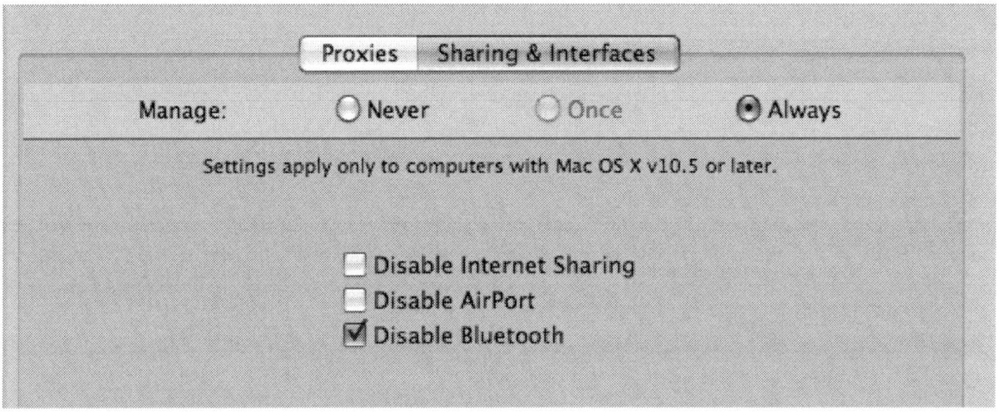

Figure 11-7. *Disabling Bluetooth via Network preferences*

As you can see, management of Bluetooth is limited and inflexible. If you just need Bluetooth to be turned off by default, but you want to allow users to turn it back on if actually needed, Apple's preference management is of no help here. You'd need to resort to a single-run script that turned Bluetooth off.

Implementing such a script is beyond the scope of this book, but one way to do this is via a post-flight script in a payload-free Installer package.

The script might look something like this:

```
#!/bin/sh
# this is designed to be run as a postflight script of a
# payload-free installer package.
# run this on Leopard or later, please.

# turn off Bluetooth
BLUETOOTHDOMAIN="$3/Library/Preferences/com.apple.Bluetooth"
defaults write "$BLUETOOTHDOMAIN " ControllerPowerState 0
defaults write "$BLUETOOTHDOMAIN " DiscoverableState 0
defaults write "$BLUETOOTHDOMAIN " BluetoothAutoSeekHIDDevices -bool False
```

```
if [ "$3" == "/" ]; then
    # we're installing on the boot volume
    # restart bluetooth daemon to pick up our changes
    killall -HUP blued
fi
```

You can find a template for a payload-free package here:

`http://managingosx.wordpress.com/2010/02/18/payload-free-package-template/`

Security Preferences

The next set of recipes covers items that, if you were to configure them manually, would be done via the Security pane in System Preferences. It is very common to manage at least some of these in an enterprise environment because of their security focus. We'll look at managing screen saver activation under both Leopard and Snow Leopard, enforcing FileVault-protected home directories, and implementing secure virtual memory.

Screen Saver

Managing the screen saver is a common security step: many organizations would like the screen saver to come on after a period of inactivity, but, more importantly, require a password to clear the screen saver. This provides a measure of protection against unauthorized people snooping around on an unattended computer.

In Leopard, after you add the preference manifests in `/System/Library/CoreServices/ManagedClient.app`, a "Screen Saver (com.apple.screensaver.ByHost)" item becomes available in the Preferences Details editor in Workgroup Manager. But to enforce requiring a password when clearing the screen saver, you'll need to do a little more work.

First, manually configure "Require Password" in the Security pane of System Preferences. Next, import the `com.apple.screensaver.xxxxxxxxxxx.plist` file from `Library/Preferences/ByHost/` in the user home directory, making sure to de-select "Import as ByHost preferences" before importing. The result is two preference domains for the Screen Saver in the Preferences Details view in Workgroup Manager. One will be labeled "com.apple.screensaver (com.apple.screensaver)," and the other will be the "Screen Saver (com.apple.screensaver.ByHost)" preferences domain that is part of the ManagedClient.app preference manifests. Figure 11-8 shows both preference domains as they should appear in Workgroup Manager.

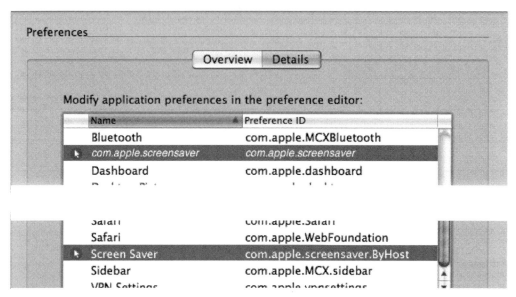

Figure 11-8. *Screen Saver preferences*

Double-click the com.apple.screensaver domain, and make sure it looks like Figure 11-9.

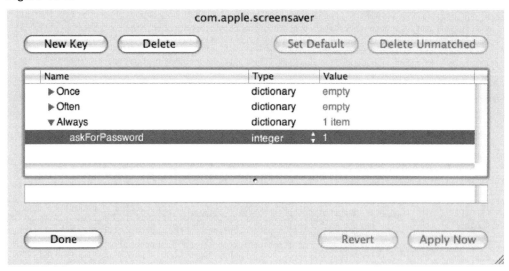

Figure 11-9. *com.apple.screensaver preferences*

Finally, double-click the com.apple.screensaver.ByHost domain, and make sure it looks like Figure 11-10.

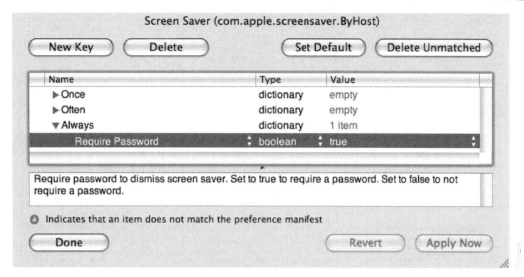

Figure 11-10. *com.apple.screensaver.ByHost preferences*

NOTE: The ManagedClient preference manifests (covered in Chapter 10) would lead you to think that you needed to manage only com.apple.screensaver.ByHost, but in practice you'll need to manage both preference domains to get the password behavior you want under Leopard.

Fortunately, this is more straightforward in Snow Leopard, and we'll look at that shortly.

If you'd like to manage the actual screen saver module and the activation time, you can do this in the com.apple.screensaver.ByHost domain, but you'll have to do it with a frequency of "Often." "Always" doesn't work, unfortunately. The downside of managing these preferences "Often" is that users can change them during their current login setting. They will be reset at the next login, however. An example is shown in Figure 11-11.

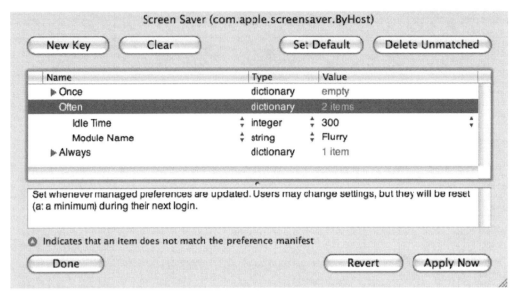

Figure 11-11. *Managing the Screen Saver module and activation time*

Managing the Screen Saver in Snow Leopard

Some of the quirks of managing the screen saver have been ironed out in Snow Leopard, and some new options have been added.

First, if you are managing the "Require password" setting, you can import the preference manifests from ManagedClient.app, and make your settings in the com.apple.screensaver domain. There's no longer a need to also manage the com.apple.ByHost domain.

Secondly, Apple added a new feature to the Security preference pane to set a delay after sleep or screen saver activation before the password is required. If you manage the "Require password" setting, you should also manage the delay. Unfortunately, the imported preference manifests do not list the appropriate key for this.

To manage this preference, we begin by setting it manually in the Security preference pane, as shown in Figure 11-12. By examining the `com.apple.screensaver.plist` file after setting this preference manually, we can determine the key we're looking for is called "askForPasswordDelay."

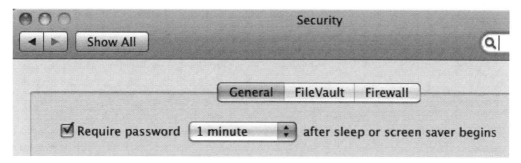

Figure 11-12. *Require password and its delay in Snow Leopard*

In Workgroup Manager, choose the Screen Saver Loginwindow (com.apple.screensaver) preference domain, and add the Require Password key. To manage the askForPasswordDelay key, just add a new key, click its name, and choose Edit. This allows us to add key names that aren't in the preference manifest. You can type askForPasswordDelay as the name of the key. Change its type to Integer, and for the value, type the number of seconds you'd like as the delay before a password is required. When you're done, it should look like Figure 11-13. Note the "Name doesn't match preference manifest" warning—we can ignore this since we added this key intentionally.

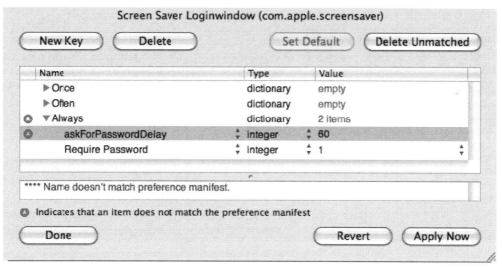

Figure 11-13. *Managing the screen saver password and its delay*

FileVault

Many large organizations require encryption of user data on mobile devices to decrease the risk of sensitive data disclosure should a device be lost or stolen.

Mac OS X offers FileVault—a technology that encrypts a user's home directory via encrypted disk images. This is not as comprehensive as a "whole-disk encryption" solution, one that encrypts everything on a startup disk. While FileVault does encrypt a user's home folder, users may still store sensitive data in other locations; for example in /Users/Shared, or in other writable directories outside of their home directory. Whole-disk encryption can cover these areas as well. But whole-disk encryption can also have its downsides, and FileVault is often an acceptable and sometimes a preferable approach. It certainly has the advantage of being included with the operating system at no additional cost.

We'll now present recipes for automating the creation of FileVault-protected home directories for both mobile users and purely-local users.

FileVault for Mobile Users

If you are already managing mobile accounts (accounts that are locally-cached copies of network accounts) on Mac OS X, it's easy to also require that on creation, these accounts are protected with FileVault.

In Workgroup Manager, select the user, group, computer, or computer group you wish to manage, click the Preferences icon, and select the Mobility preferences. Under Account Creation, click the "Options" tab, and you should see a set of controls like those in Figure 11-14.

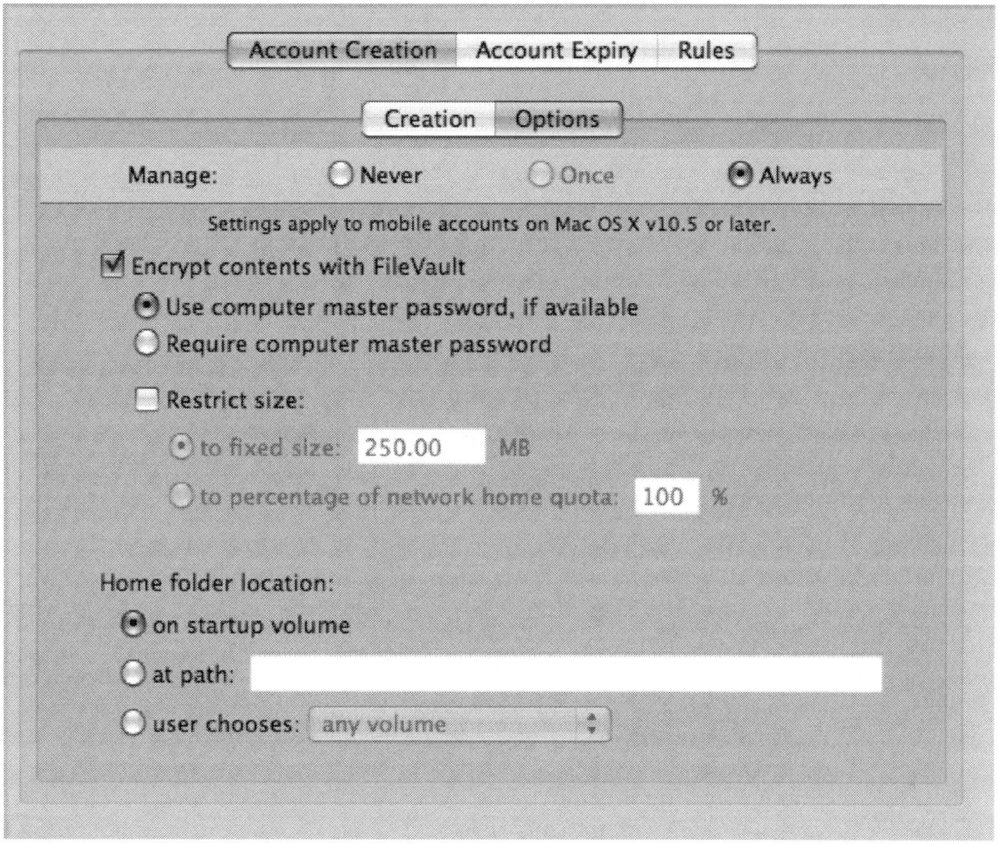

Figure 11-14. *Workgroup Manager Mobility Account Creation Options pane*

Since these preferences are applied when creating mobile accounts, "Never" and "Always" are the only frequency options that make sense.

Checking "Encrypt contents with FileVault" causes all new mobile accounts to be created with FileVault turned on—the user is not given a choice in the matter.

In an enterprise environment, it is also common to use a managed FileVault master password to allow password and data recovery if the account password is lost. In the Action Creation Options pane, this password is referred to as a "computer master password." Selecting "Require computer master password" prevents the creation of FileVault-protected accounts without a FileVault master password in place. Unfortunately, there is no method using MCX to manage the actual FileVault master password.

Fortunately, it's fairly simple to manage the FileVault master password without MCX. Just set the master password on one machine, and then copy the following two files to all your managed machines:

`/Library/Keychains/FileVaultMaster.cer`

`/Library/Keychains/FileVaultMaster.keychain`

Note that you must do this before creating any mobile accounts on a given machine; adding or changing these files later does not retroactively change the FileVault master password for an account created earlier.

FileVault for Local Users

If you are protecting mobile account data on laptops by using FileVault, it makes sense to extend that protection to purely local accounts. Rather than making it an organizational policy to be sure to turn on FileVault for all local accounts on laptops, you want to use the managed preferences system to make it automatic, just like for mobile accounts.

Unfortunately, Workgroup Manager provides no obvious way to enforce this particular preference. But don't worry—you can manage this by importing preferences from the System Preferences application.

You'll need to use the "Details" view in the Preferences editor in Workgroup Manager to directly manage specific preferences. This preference makes sense only at the computer or computer group level (since you are managing a setting relevant to the computer as a whole, and not a particular user). Choose a computer or computer group to manage, click the Preferences icon in the toolbar, and then select the Details pane. Click the "+" button to add a new preference domain. Navigate to `/Applications` and double-click the System Preferences app. The results should look something like Figure 11-15.

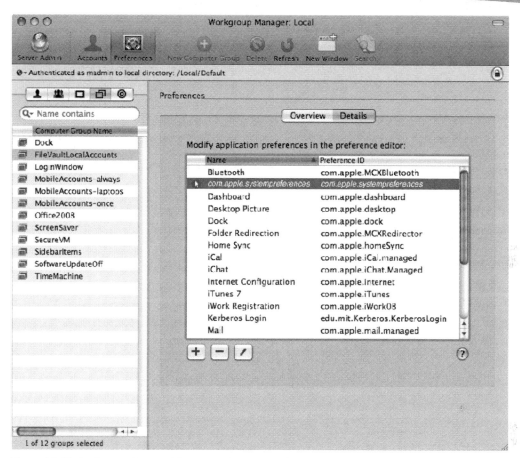

Figure 11-15. *Preferences imported for com.apple.systempreferences*

Double-click the entry for com.apple.systempreferences and delete all the imported keys—you don't want any of them, as none of them are related to managing FileVault. Expand the "Always" dictionary, and add a new key called "com.apple.preferences. accounts.forceFVForNewUsers" with a Boolean value of `true`. Figure 11-16 shows the results.

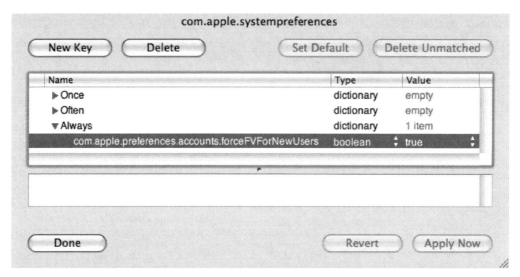

Figure 11-16. *com.apple.preferences.accounts.forceFVForNewUsers key*

Apply your changes, and log into a computer that is a member of the computer group for which you are managing this preference. Open the Accounts pane in System Preferences and attempt to create a new account. You should see that "Turn on FileVault protection" is selected and disabled, as in Figure 11-17.

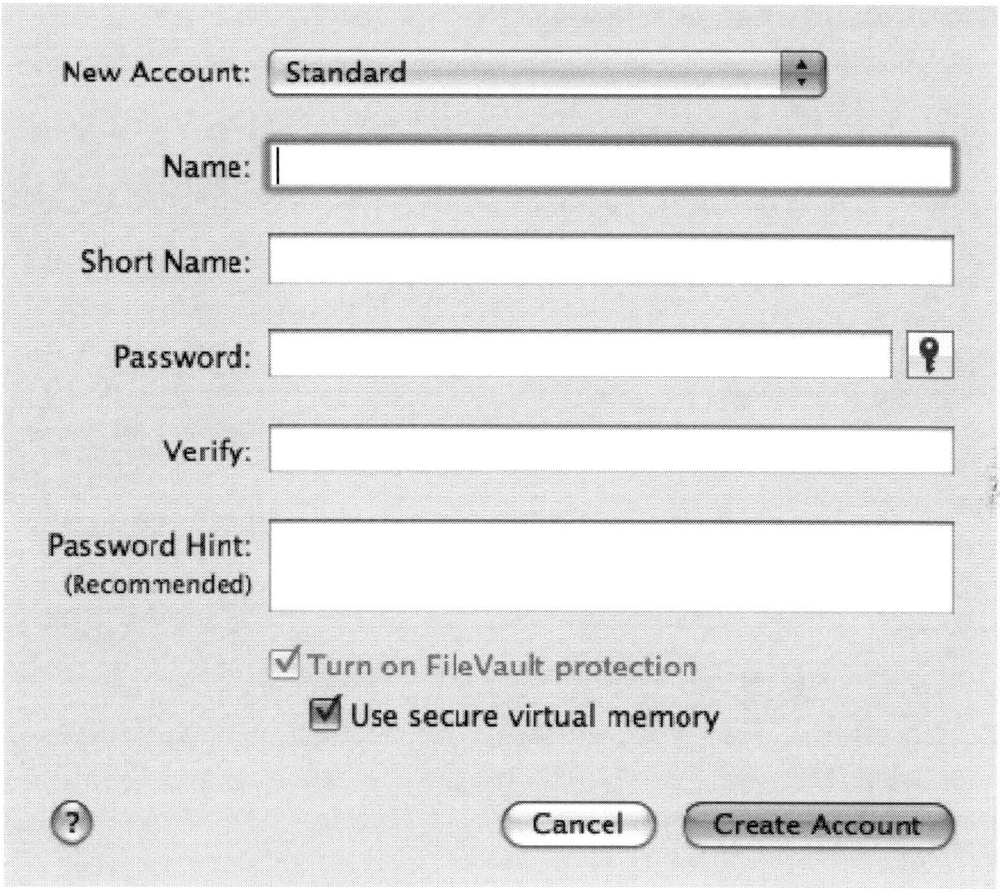

New Account:	Standard

Name: |

Short Name:

Password:

Verify:

Password Hint:
(Recommended)

☑ Turn on FileVault protection
☑ Use secure virtual memory

(?)   (Cancel) (Create Account)

Figure 11-17. *Enforced FileVault for new local accounts*

Secure Virtual Memory

If you are securing laptop user data with FileVault, you should consider securing the virtual memory swap file. This file contains data temporarily swapped out from RAM, and so could contain user data. Encrypting this file makes it less likely that a thief could find anything of interest.

Again, Workgroup Manger does not provide an obvious way to manage this preference, so you'll need to use a technique similar to the one we used to manage FileVault for local accounts. The preference domain is "com.apple.virtualMemory," and the preference key is "UseEncryptedSwap."

Via the command line, it looks like this:

dscl /Search mcxread /ComputerGroups/managed_laptops com.apple.virtualMemory

Key: UseEncryptedSwap

State: always

Value: 1

In Workgroup Manager, it looks like Figure 11-18.

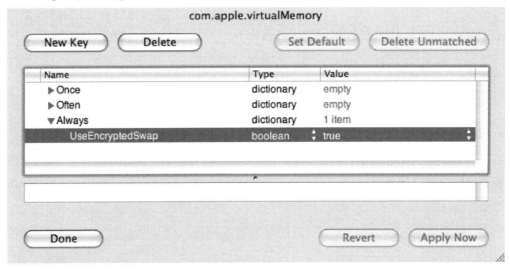

Figure 11-18. *Managing encrypted virtual memory*

Managing iTunes

iTunes is an important part of the Mac experience, at least from Apple's viewpoint. One could argue that it has no place on a "business" computer, and you may be tempted to remove it from all the computers you manage. With any luck, you and your organization aren't that draconian. So if you leave iTunes on your managed Macs, you may want to manage certain features of iTunes to make it easier to support, or to disable functionality that might be inappropriate for your organization. It's not uncommon for organizations to disable shared music, or block access to the iTunes Store, to prevent users from buying and downloading music onto company-owned computers. If your organization has usage policies that apply to applications like iTunes, you might want to manage at least some iTunes preferences.

When you import the preference manifests from /System/Library/CoreServices/ ManagedClient.app under Leopard or Snow Leopard, you get a preference manifest for iTunes. It does contain a number of useful keys to manage, as shown in Figure 11-19.

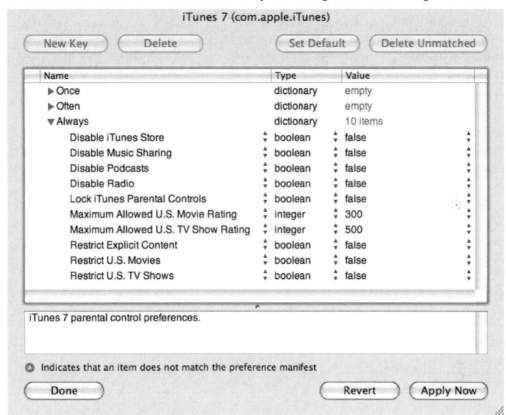

Figure 11-19. *iTunes preference manifest available preferences*

But there are more preferences you can manage; you'll need to add them manually from the list in Table 11-1.

Table 11-1. *Additional iTunes Preferences to Manage*

Preference Key	Type	Where to find in iTunes preferences	Notes
allowiTunesUAccess	Boolean	Parental Control	
disableAppleTV	Boolean	Apple TV	
disableAutomaticDeviceSync	Boolean	Devices	"Prevent … from syncing"
disableCheckForUpdates	Boolean	General	See following note
disableDeviceRegistration	Boolean	Devices	
disableGeniusSidebar	Boolean	General	
disableGetAlbumArtwork	Boolean	Store	
disableMusicStore	Boolean	Parental Control	
disablePodcasts	Boolean	Parental Control	
disableRadio	Boolean	Parental Control	
disableSharedMusic	Boolean	Parental Control	
gamesLimit	integer	Parental Control	See following note
moviesLimit	integer	Parental Control	See following note
restrictExplicit	Boolean	Parental Control	
restrictMovies	Boolean	Parental Control	
restrictTVShows	Boolean	Parental Control	
ratingSystemID	integer	Parental Control	"Ratings for:"
restrictGames	Boolean	Parental Control	Content Restrictions: Applications
tvShowsLimit	integer	Parental Control	See following note

NOTE: If you set "disableCheckForUpdates" to `true`, this also turns off checking for iPhone/iPod touch software updates and disables the ability to restore the software on an iPhone/iPod touch (at least through iTunes version 9.1.1.)

The integer values for "gamesLimit," "moviesLimit," and "tvShowsLimit" are seemingly arbitrary, but control the limits selected in the related pop-up menus in the iTunes Parental Control preferences. Since what is displayed in these menus depends on which country's ratings system you are using, you will have to experiment with setting the values to what you want using iTunes' preferences dialog, and then using *defaults read com.apple.iTunes <preferencekey>* to discover the value you need.

Even though many of these keys are not in the iTunes 7 preference manifest, you can add them manually if you need to manage them. To add a key, click "Always" in the Name column and click the "New Key" button. An item named "New Item" will appear in the list. Click its name and a pop-up menu will appear—choose the "Edit" item. Type the name of the new key you'd like to add. Click the type to change the type to Boolean or integer as applicable, and finally set the value as desired. Ignore the "Name doesn't match preference manifest" warning.

NOTE: We covered preference manifests in Chapter 10. They can help administrators discover useful preference keys to manage, but they rarely contain every possible key you can manage. If you add a key to the management list for a preference domain that is not in the preference manifest (if there is one), you'll see a warning. This warning doesn't mean that what you are trying to manage won't work; it means only that the key is not in the manifest.

Figure 11-20 has an example of a preference manifest key and a manually added key.

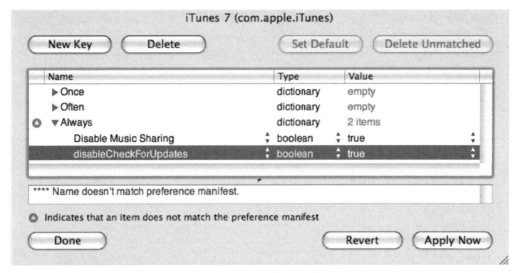

Figure 11-20. *Adding an additional iTunes preference key with manifest warning*

Managing Office 2008

So far, we've focused on managing preferences for elements of the operating system, or Apple applications. But any application that stores its preferences as standard `.plist` files in the user's `Library/Preferences` folder is a candidate for management.

As an example, we'll look at Microsoft Office 2008. Many of the Office 2008 applications now use `.plist` files to store their preferences. (A major exception is Entourage, which still stores a lot of its preferences in the monolithic Entourage database.) The use of `.plist` files means we can use the managed preferences system to manage many of Office 2008's preferences.

Here are some Office 2008 preferences you might want to manage in an enterprise environment:

- Default save file formats
- Microsoft AutoUpdate checks
- Office Setup Assistant

To manage these preferences, we'll use Workgroup Manager to import the `.plist` files, and then edit the MCX settings that result.

Default Save File Formats

One of the management challenges with Microsoft Office is that different versions of Office use different file formats. While newer versions of Office can usually read and write the older file formats without issues, the converse is not true. Once you've upgraded a few users to a newer version of Office, you may start running into support issues because the users of the new version of Office are creating documents in the new file format versions. Therefore, you might want configure the Office 2008 applications to save to the older Office 97–2004 formats by default. This will maximize compatibility with users in your organization who are still using older versions of Office.

Start by opening each application and making the preference changes you want, and then quit each app in turn. So, open Microsoft Word; open its Preferences dialog, and in the Save pane, set "Save Word files" to "Word 97–2007 Document (.doc)." See Figure 11-21 for an example.

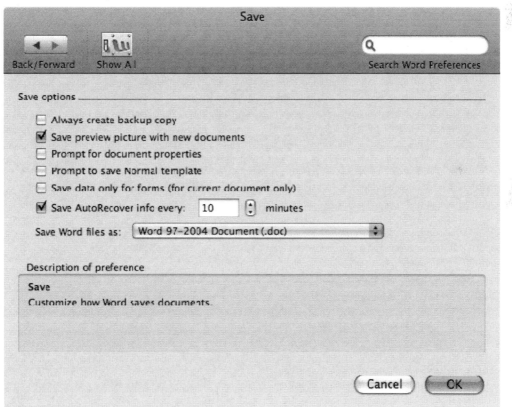

Figure 11-21. *Microsoft Word 2008 Save preferences*

Click OK and quit Microsoft Word. Repeat with Excel and Powerpoint, making the equivalent changes to the Save settings for these applications.

Microsoft AutoUpdate

If you are managing software updates for your organization, you may not want AutoUpdate alerting your users as well.

Microsoft AutoUpdate can be found in /Library/Application Support/Microsoft/ MAU2.0/. Open it and set it to check for updates manually, as in Figure 11-22. This turns off the automatic, periodic check. Now it will run only when a user specifically checks for updates manually.

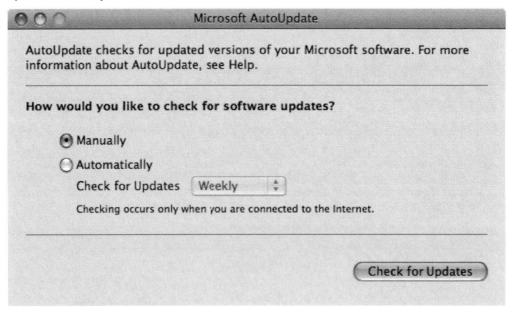

Figure 11-22. *Microsoft AutoUpdate*

Office Setup Assistant

Microsoft Office 2008 has a Setup Assistant that runs on first launch after installation. This assistant walks the user through some initial setup tasks and prompts them register, among other things. Presumably as the systems administrator, you've already performed many or most of these tasks, and so do not want to bother your end-users with this Assistant.

After installing Office 2008, let the Setup Assistant run once (or run it manually from `/Applications/Microsoft Office 2008/Office/`) and set things up as appropriate for your organization. Then take our word for it that the preference you need to manage is stored in `~/Library/Preferences/com.microsoft.office.plist` under the key "2008\FirstRun\SetupAssistCompleted". We'll import that `.plist` file in a moment.

Importing Office Preferences for Management

Now that we've manually configured our desired preferences for the various Office applications, we're ready to import them into Workgroup Manager so we can manage them. Open Workgroup Manager and create a new computer group called "Office2008" (you may choose to do this at a workgroup level instead). Click the Preferences icon, and then the "Details" tab.

Click the "+" button and import the following `.plist` files:

`~/Library/Preferences/com.microsoft.Excel.plist`

`~/Library/Preferences/com.microsoft.Powerpoint.plist`

`~/Library/Preferences/com.microsoft.Word.plist`

`~/Library/Preferences/com.microsoft.autoupdate2.plist`

`~/Library/Preferences/com.microsoft.office.plist`

You can't import them all at once; you'll need to import each `.plist` file one by one. As you import each one, you are given the choice of importing the preferences as "Once," "Often," or "Always."

Apple warns that "Always" may not work with third-party applications, and that "Often" is often the better choice. If you want your users to be able to change the default save format, import the Word, Excel, and PowerPoint preferences as "Once." The other two you should import as "Often," which causes MCX to re-apply the desired preferences at each login.

When you are done importing, it should look like Figure 11-23.

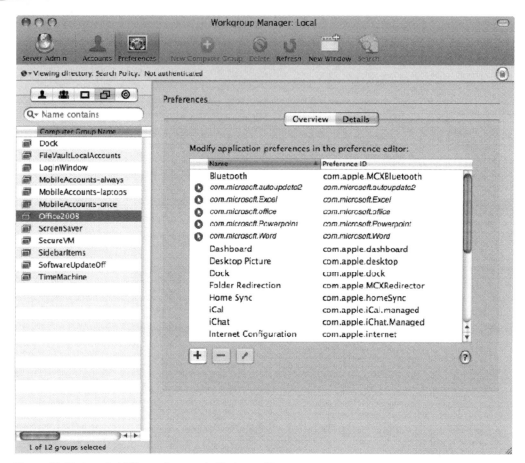

Figure 11-23. *Imported Office preferences in Workgroup Manager*

Unfortunately, when you import preferences this way, you get everything that's currently in the .plist file. Simply delete the preferences you aren't interested in managing, but be careful not to delete the ones you want to keep! If you make a mistake, just import the original .plist file and try again.

The Word preferences after deleting everything except the default save format key are shown in Figure 11-24.

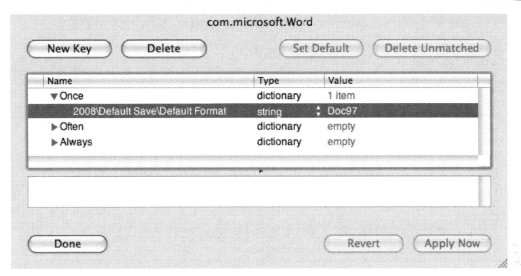

Figure 11-24. *Managed Microsoft Word 2008 preferences*

Managed preferences for Microsoft AutoUpdate are shown in Figure 11-25.

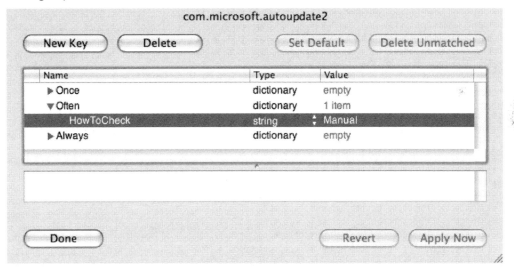

Figure 11-25. *Managed Microsoft AutoUpdate preferences*

Here are the preference keys for the other Microsoft applications we've discussed:

com.microsoft.Excel:

2008\Default Save\Default Format

Value: 57

State: once

com.microsoft.Powerpoint:

2008\Default Save\Default Save\Default Format

Value: Microsoft PowerPoint 98 Presentation

State: once

com.microsoft.office:

2008\FirstRun\SetupAssistCompleted

Value: 1

State: often

Summary

We presented "recipes"—step-by-step directions—for common preferences that system administrators typically want to manage. These recipes can be used directly, but we hope that they serve as guides for other preferences you want to manage.

Managing the items that appear in, and in appearance of, the Finder sidebar is an example of preference management done to improve the user experience for your organization.

Implementing security policies is another common use of managed preferences; we presented recipes for more secure configurations of the login window, Bluetooth, the Screen Saver, FileVault, and secure virtual memory.

Some organizations have "appropriate use" policies, where users are expected to use IT resources in a manner appropriate for an organization. Managed preferences can help users comply with these policies. We looked at some ways to restrict some of the features of Apple's iTunes application to help users comply with organizational policies.

Finally, we demonstrated using managed preferences to provide a better user experience for Microsoft Office 2008 and to help avoid issues with file format incompatibilities between different versions of Office. This is an example of using Apple's Managed Preferences framework to manage third-party applications.

Chapter **12**

Managing Mobile Accounts

A very common use for managed preferences on Mac OS X is to manage mobile accounts. In fact, it was precisely this need that caused one of your humble authors to implement Local MCX in his organization—he had previously managed a lot of things through the use of various scripts that directly manipulated preference files. But a desire to automate the creation of mobile accounts and the enforcement of FileVault protection for these accounts led him to implement managed preferences. This then trickled down and replaced most of the homegrown management scripts used earlier.

Apple has provided many useful controls for configuring and controlling the creation and management of mobile accounts in their Managed Preferences framework. Many of the things that are relatively straightforward to implement using Managed Preferences are difficult if not impossible to implement any other way.

Chapter 11 contains several small, self-contained recipes for using managed preferences to address common administrative tasks. This chapter can be thought of as a bigger recipe devoted to a single subject, mobile accounts. We'll explore using managed preferences to simplify the creation of mobile accounts, the enforcement of FileVault security, and the setup of HomeSync preferences. We'll also discuss some of the major choices to consider when implementing a management policy for mobile accounts.

Mobile Accounts Review

You may remember that a mobile account is a user account whose information originates in a network directory service, but is cached in the local directory service. This provides the benefits of a network account, such as centralized administration, consistent access to internal network resources, and the same username and password regardless of machine. However, since the account information is cached locally on the machine, a user can still log in and use the computer even if it's not connected to the organization's network. Changes in the network account information are synchronized with the locally cached account, and vice versa.

Mobile accounts are especially useful on laptops, which, due to their nature, are frequently not on the organization's network. In the past, laptops were difficult to manage with management systems that relied on a continuously available network connection. This was less of a problem when laptops were relatively uncommon. But today, laptops are a larger percentage of machines in many organizations, making it increasingly important to develop and implement effective management strategies. Because they may regularly leave the premises of your organization, laptops introduce new things to worry about, making consistently managing these devices even more important.

Prerequisites

There are certain prerequisites for mobile accounts. Most importantly, you must have a network directory service already in place. In most cases, you'll also want to have network home directories available. Setting up a network account/network home infrastructure is beyond the scope of this book. But if your organization already has in place a network directory service such as Open Directory, Active Directory, or an LDAPv3 directory, you should be able to configure mobile accounts, using this chapter as a guide.

> **NOTE:** For best results, if you are using an LDAPv3 directory you may need to extend the LDAP schema to include the apple-generateduid attribute for all user objects (and index this attribute as well!). Refer to Chapter 6 for more information about LDAP schema extension.

If, in addition, user accounts in the network directory service have network home directories, you can also create "portable home directories," in which a subset of the network home is kept in sync with a local home directory.

Definitions

Let's step back a bit and discuss three terms that sometimes get mashed up: mobile accounts, portable home directories, and HomeSync.

Mobile Accounts

The term "mobile accounts" refers to the actual account itself: a locally cached copy of account information that originates from a network directory service. The local account information is kept in sync with the network account information. Mobile accounts have local home directories; these local home directories may or may not be synchronized with a network home.

Portable Home Directories

Portable home directories is Apple's term for local home directories that are synchronized with a network home. They require a mobile account. Mobile accounts and portable home directories can be of use even on desktop machines. Since they have a local home directory, they are a solution for issues with applications that are not compatible with network home directories. Local home directories can also provide a performance boost, especially in organizations with slow networks.

HomeSync

HomeSync is the process that makes portable home directories possible. It keeps the local home directory and network home directory in sync, using synchronization rules that specify which folders to synchronize and any exceptions or exclusions. It can run at login, logout, periodically in the background, and on user demand.

Manual Setup of Mobile Accounts

Let's begin by walking through a *manual* setup of a mobile account, so that we can see some of the issues around mobile accounts, portable home directories, and HomeSync. We'll start by assuming the client Mac is already connected to a network directory service, and that network users are able to log in.

First, log in using a network account. While logged in, open the System Preferences application and choose the Accounts pane. Unlock the pane by clicking the padlock in the lower left corner and providing the credentials of an administrator. Figure 12-1 shows the result so far.

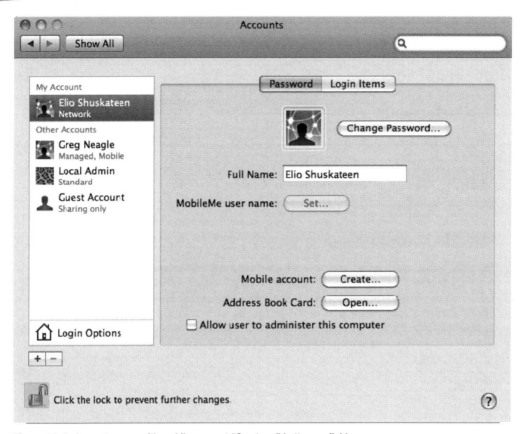

Figure 12-1. *Accounts pane with mobile account "Create..." button available*

Next, click the mobile account "Create..." button. A dialog like the one in Figure 12-2 will appear.

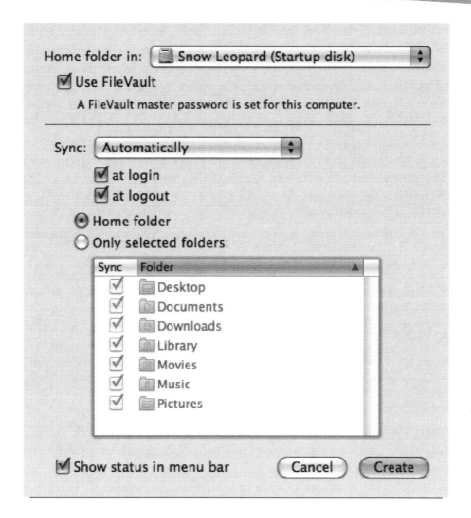

Figure 12-2. *Mobile account creation dialog*

A variety of options are now available, enabling you to

- Choose where to create the local home folder, if there are multiple volumes available

NOTE: "Folder" and "directory" are synonyms in most cases; you'll see these terms used interchangeably in many contexts.

- Enable FileVault
- Specify the frequency of periodic synchronization, and whether synchronization occurs at login and/or logout

- Choose to sync the entire home folder, or just a subset of folders in the home

- Choose whether to show the HomeSync status in the menu bar

As we've just seen, we can create and configure mobile accounts manually, but there are some issues. The first is that we need administrative credentials to unlock the button that allows us to create a mobile account from the currently logged-in network account. This might mean that you'll need a support person to assist. Second, the number of available options when creating a mobile account makes consistent setup difficult. When mobile accounts are set up manually, they may not always be set up with the same options. Finally, the controls for choosing which items are synchronized are not very flexible. There is no way to specify exceptions to the synchronization; you can only choose to sync the entire home folder, or a subset of the top-level folders within the home folder.

To deal with some of these issues, you must turn to Managed Preferences. Managed Preferences can help with mobile account setup and configuration, and they provide more precise control of HomeSync options than is found in the Mobile Account Preferences pane (shown in Figure 12-2) available to regular end-users.

Automatic Setup of Mobile Accounts

In an enterprise environment, manually setting up mobile accounts for every computer that needs them would consume a lot of time and effort. This is the sort of task an enterprise systems administrator would want to automate as much as possible. Using Apple's Managed Preferences is the best way to accomplish this goal.

Using Managed Preferences, we can configure a group of machines so that

- On first login with their network accounts, users are asked if they'd like to create a mobile account.

- If the user agrees, a mobile account is created. The local home directory is protected with FileVault.

- The mobile account is initially and consistently set up with synchronization settings appropriate to our organization.

With such a configuration, we should no longer need a technician to configure mobile accounts for our users; instead they should be able to log in to a new laptop and it will be configured for them.

Configuring Managed Preferences for Mobile Users

Before we begin actually setting up the managed preferences, we should take a moment and decide exactly at what level we should manage these settings. One logical choice would be to create a computer group containing all (or a subset of) the laptop computers in your organization. With this configuration, we will be able to set things up so that when any user logs into a laptop, he or she is prompted to create a mobile account (or have a mobile account created without asking). If that same user logs into a desktop machine, he or she will get his or her network home directory.

The other choice would be to manage mobile user preferences for a specific group of users. For these users, no matter what computer they logged into, they would get a mobile account (or at least the option to create one).

If your users log into only a single computer, and each computer has only a single user (a "one-to-one deployment," common in many businesses), both arrangements are essentially the same, and you could choose to manage mobile accounts via computer groups or groups of users.

If you assign laptops to certain users, but these same users occasionally log into desktop machines, then managing mobile accounts via computer groups is probably a better choice. This way they can have a mobile account when they log into their laptops, but a network account and network home when they log into a desktop Mac.

With either arrangement, you can handle special cases by adding managed mobile account settings to a specific computer or user account as needed.

For the discussions in this chapter, we'll add our managed mobile account settings to computer groups, but if a group of users makes more sense in your environment, feel free to use that instead. You can also mix and match, but remember the rules of MCX precedence: computer groups have a higher precedence than groups of users.

For maximum flexibility, we'll separate our mobile account settings into three groupings. Each of these groupings will be assigned to a separate computer group or group of users (depending on your preference):

- *Mobile Account Creation:* These are the preferences that control the initial creation of mobile accounts. These can be managed only "Never" (that is, not managed at all) or "Always."

- *Mobile Account Expiration:* These are preferences that allow you to automatically remove mobile accounts from a machine after a certain amount of time. Like the Account Creation settings, these can be managed only "Never" or "Always."

- *Home Synchronization settings:* These dictate what gets synchronized and when. Sync rules can be managed "Never," "Once," or "Always."

Depending on your environment and users, you may not need all of these groupings. The advantage of having these separate groupings is that you could, for example, make mobile account creation mandatory on one group of machines, optional, but still managed, on another group of machines, and completely manual on another group of machines. For all of these machines, though, you could manage synchronization in the same way, so that if a mobile account is manually created on a desktop machine, it behaves the same way as a mobile account automatically created on a laptop. Having separate computer groups for these preference groupings allows you to more easily mix and match preference management for different sets of machines.

Let's take a deeper look at each grouping of managed preferences.

Mobile Account Creation

In Workgroup Manager, start by creating a computer group named "MobileAccountCreation." Switch to the Preferences Overview by clicking the Preferences icon in the toolbar. See Figure 12-3 for an illustration.

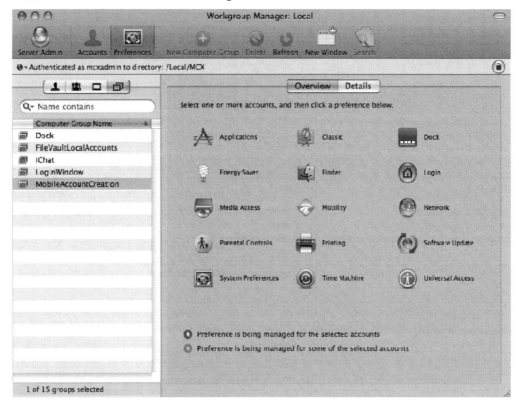

Figure 12-3. *Workgroup Manager Preferences Overview*

In the Preferences Overview, click the Mobility icon. The pane will change to a set of managed preferences editors, as shown in Figure 12-4. If necessary, select the "Account Creation" and "Creation" tabs.

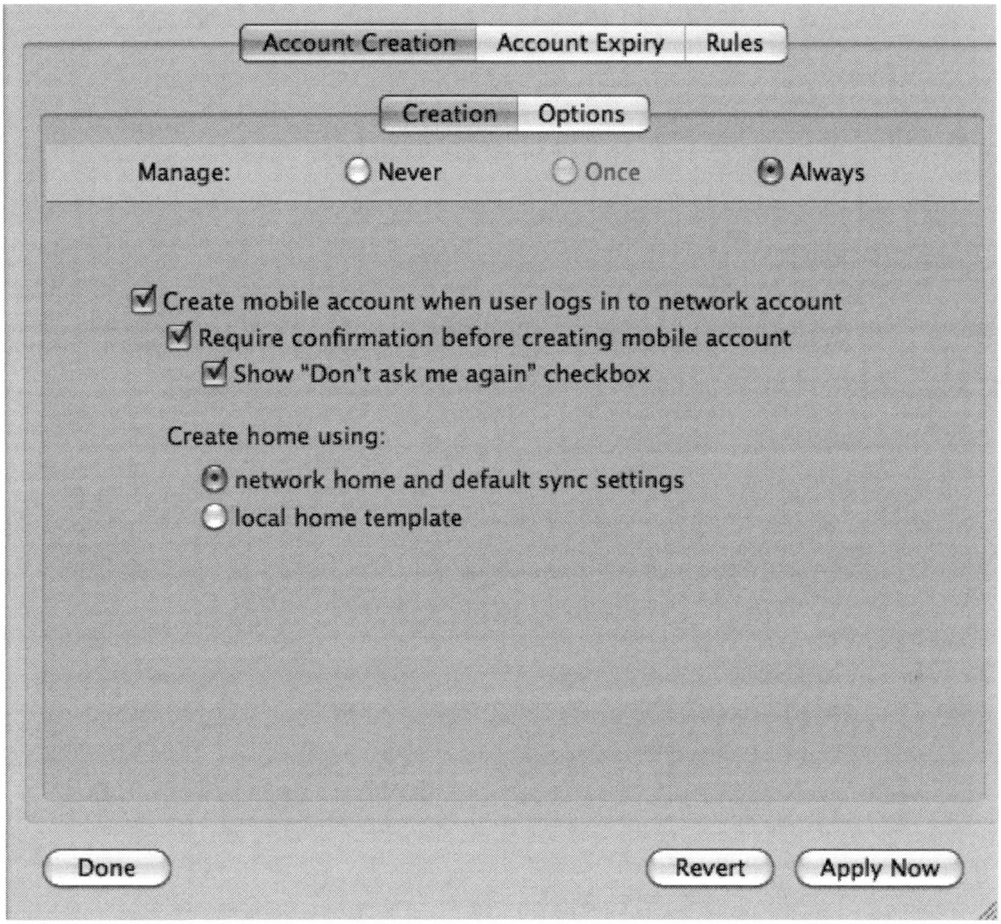

Figure 12-4. *Mobile Account Creation preferences editor*

Choose to manage these preferences "Always," and select "Create mobile account when user logs in to network account." Now the choices begin:

■ If "Require confirmation before creating mobile account" is checked, the user will be asked if he or she wants to create a mobile account when the user logs in using his or her network account. If you'd like the account to be automatically created without asking, uncheck this.

■ The "Show 'Don't ask me again' check box" allows users to turn off the mobile account confirmation dialog for future logins. If they don't check "Don't ask me again," or you don't enable this option, users will be asked at every network login if they want to create a mobile account.

■ If you select "Create home using: network home and default sync settings," when a mobile account is created, the local home will be created based on the current contents of the network home and the Mac OS X default sync settings will be applied (if no other sync settings are managed). This is a good choice if you plan to support portable home directories.

■ Selecting "Create home using: local home template" causes the local home to be set up the same way a home directory is initially set up for new local-only users. Unless you have managed synchronization rules, there will be no home synchronization. This is the option to choose if you do not want the local home synchronized with a network home.

NOTE: Consider carefully the consequences of your choices in this pane. In our environment, we require confirmation on creation. This allows the primary user of a laptop to create a mobile account, but also allows other users, especially support personnel, to be able to log in without necessarily creating a mobile account. On the other hand, creating a mobile account without confirmation on laptops is probably the right thing to do most of the time, and avoids either an extra call to the help desk or the end-user making the "wrong" choice.

If you are managing the creation of mobile accounts in user groups instead of computer groups, you could have a group of "regular" users who get a mobile account automatically when logging in, and, for your group of tech support personnel, require confirmation before creating a mobile account.

Once you've made your choices here, click the tab control labeled "Options." You'll see a set of controls like those in Figure 12-5.

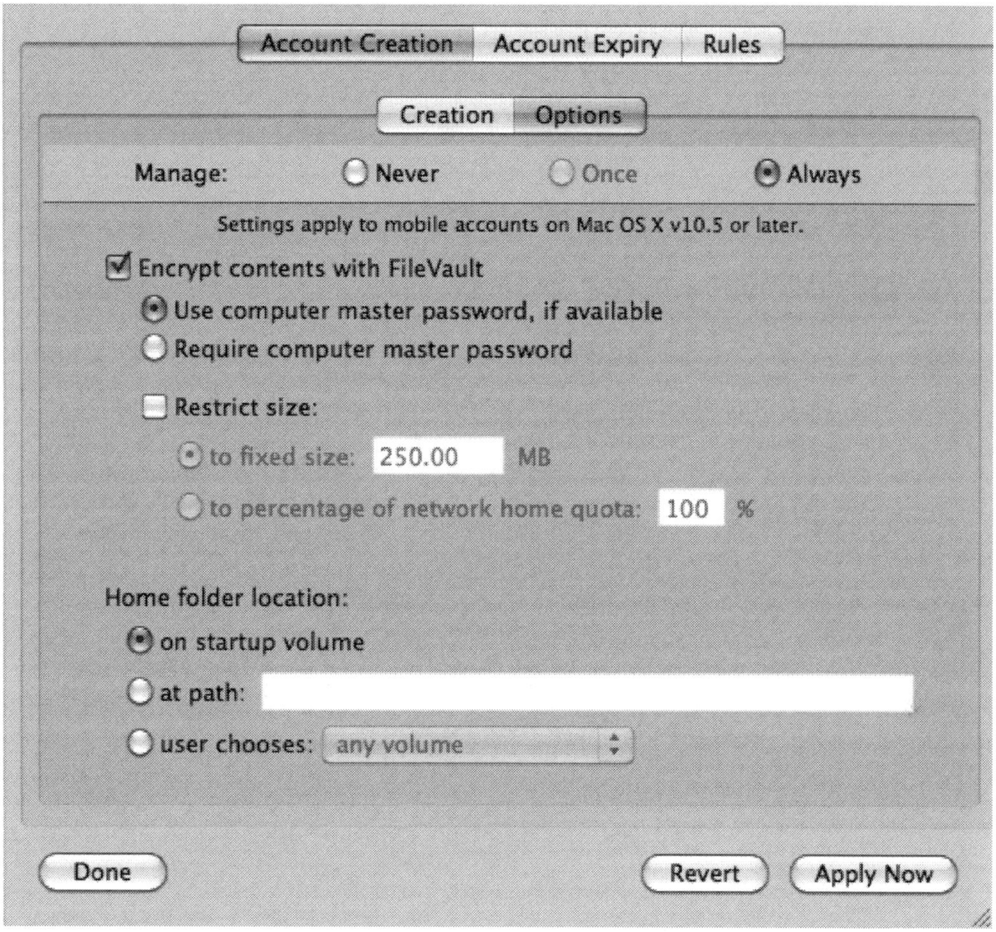

Figure 12-5. *Mobile Account Creation Options pane*

We discussed the FileVault options in Chapter 10, so we won't repeat them here. If you do choose to encrypt with FileVault, since the contents of the local home are stored in a disk image, an option to restrict the size becomes available. You can restrict the size to either a fixed number of megabytes, or a percentage of the network home quota. This can be useful as a way to prevent the local home from growing too large to completely sync with the network home. When we look at the synchronization rules, we'll also see another strategy for dealing with potentially large local homes: excluding certain folders from the synchronization.

The last set of choices here is the location of the local home. By default, the local home is created in the familiar Users folder of the startup disk. But you can specify an alternate path. For example, if you've partitioned the internal disk on all your Macs so there are multiple volumes, you could force the creation of the mobile account's home folder on a secondary partition. Such an arrangement makes it easier to "wipe and reinstall" a problematic machine without affecting user data, since the user data is stored on a different partition from the OS and applications.

The final choice in this set prompts the user to choose the volume for the home. The pop-up menu allows you to let the user choose any volume, or you may restrict the choices to any internal volume or any external (or removable) volume. Choosing an external volume adds an interesting new wrinkle. This type of mobile account, that is, one where the home folder is created on a removable volume, is called an "external account." This allows a user to store the home folder and account information on a removable drive—a FireWire or USB disk, or even a USB keychain drive. This can be a useful arrangement in an education environment, where the sheer number of students or the network infrastructure makes traditional network home directories problematic. For example, each student is supplied (or is required to purchase) his or her own USB keychain drive. The students connect their drives to managed computers, log in, and have access to their data. No matter which computer they use, their home directories are available, and when they leave the school, they can take their data with them.

If you want to force the creation of external accounts, select "user chooses: any external volume" for the home folder location. If you do use external accounts, give some thought to the security implications. Since it's trivial to access anything on an external disk, you may want to consider using FileVault to secure the contents of the home directory on the external volume. On the other hand, in an education environment, using FileVault might be more trouble than it is worth.

Once you've made all your choices for mobile account creation, click the "Apply Now" button. If you've made the same choices as we've shown in Figures 12-4 and 12-5, any computers added to the MobileAccountCreation computer group will have the following behaviors:

- Network users will be asked if they want to create a mobile account upon login.

- Users can check the "Don't ask me again" check box if they don't want a mobile account and don't want to be asked again in the future.

- The local home will be created based on the contents of the network home, and the default synchronization settings will be used.

- The local home will be encrypted with FileVault, and the FileVault master password will be used if it is set. (Setting a FileVault master password for all your machines was covered in Chapter 10.)

- The local home will be created on the startup volume.

- The size of the local home will not be restricted, and could grow to fill the startup volume.

Mobile Account Expiry

If you've configured your machines to create a mobile account for each network user as he or she logs in, and your users often move from machine to machine (as is common in an education or training environment), you may be faced with the problem of multiplying mobile accounts. Over time, as your users use different machines, they leave copies of their mobile accounts on each machine they use. In the worst case, eventually every machine has a mobile account for every user in your organization, filling up the startup disks on every machine. Obviously, this is not an ideal situation. Prior to the release of Mac OS X Leopard, administrators had to deal with this situation on their own, writing scripts to clean up, or visiting each machine to remove old mobile accounts.

With Mac OS X Leopard, Apple added a new feature to the management of mobile accounts: Account Expiry. Let's explore this feature.

Using Workgroup Manager, create a new computer group called "MobileAccountExpiry." Switch to the Preferences Overview and select the Mobility preferences. Refer back to Figure 12-3 if you've forgotten what the Preferences Overview looks like. After selecting the Mobility preferences, select the "Account Expiry" tab, and click "Always" in the choices to manage "Never," "Once" (which is dimmed), or "Always." See Figure 12-6 for an example.

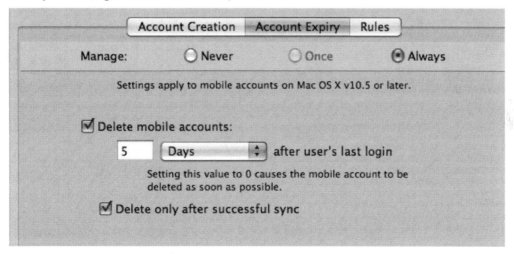

Figure 12-6. *Mobile Account Expiry options*

The options here are easy to understand; you can choose the number of hours, days, or weeks after which a mobile account will be deleted, and choose to delete only after a successful sync with the network home. This last option can help prevent user data loss—a mobile account that did not have a successful sync may have the only copy of some user data, so deleting it would cause that data to be lost. Note that this option does not mean that a sync will be attempted before deletion; instead it means that it considers the status of the synchronization that occurred when the user was last logged in. Consider using this option especially if you are very aggressive in deleting mobile accounts. If, on the other hand, you wait weeks before deleting old mobile accounts, it may be less important to ensure a successful sync before deletion.

Mobile account expiry may not be applicable to your organization at all. If you have a one-to-one deployment, where each machine has a single primary user, mobile account expiry is probably not needed.

Managing Home Synchronization

The last group of settings we can manage for mobile accounts deals with the synchronization of the local home directory and the network home directory.

Before we delve into the details of managing home synchronization, we should cover some general concepts.

There are two sets of file system items that are synchronized—preferences, and everything else in the home folder. In Workgroup Manager in Mac OS X 10.6, these sets are referred to as "Preference Sync" and "Home Sync," respectively. There are four times synchronization can happen: at login, logout, periodically in the background, and when manually started.

> **NOTE:** Originally (in Mac OS X 10.4), the preference set was synced only at login and logout, and everything else was synced during periodic and manual syncs. So in some documentation and in older versions of Workgroup Manager, you may see "Login & Logout Sync" used interchangeably with "Preferences Sync," and "Background Sync" used interchangeably with "Home Sync."

Since preference files are typically read by an application when it first launches, and are not written until the application quits, syncing these during periodic background syncs is not likely to have the desired effect for applications that are open when the sync occurs. Preference files and other files an application keeps open are best synchronized when they are not in use. Since no user-level applications are in use during the login and logout processes, this is an ideal time to synchronize these items.

Why not just synchronize everything at login and logout, since presumably no application is using files in your home at these times? While this might be a safe strategy, it increases the amount of time needed at login and logout, leading to a poorer user experience. Apple's strategy is to sync as much as possible during periodic background syncs so the user does not notice; then use login and logout syncs to synchronize only what is absolutely necessary in order to speed up the login and logout process. Keep that in mind if you decide to change what is synced at login and logout.

Each set of synchronized items—the "Preference Sync" set and the "Home Sync" set—is specified by two lists, a list of folders to be synchronized, and a list of exclusions. You can use managed preferences to specify the contents of these lists and thus customize exactly what is synchronized.

You can also use managed preferences to specify how often background syncs occur, and which sets ("Preference Sync" and "Home Sync") are synchronized at login, logout, in the background, and manually.

> **NOTE:** These options are available in Mac OS X 10.6. If you are using Mac OS X 10.5 or earlier, you have less precise control over these combinations.

All of the options available through managed preferences allow you great flexibility in customizing home synchronization. However, the controls available to the end-user are much more limited, as we saw in Figure 12-2 when configuring a mobile account manually. This means that if you want to allow the user to be able to make changes to the Mobile Account preferences, you may not be able to use some of the managed preferences options, because doing so will either prevent user changes, or cause what the user sees in the Mobile Accounts preferences dialog to not match the effective settings, leading to user confusion, and in the worst case, data loss, as we'll explain next.

Synchronization Management Strategies

To deal with some of the issues just raised, we can recommend four possible strategies for managing synchronization.

- *Stick with the defaults*: The first strategy is to specify no managed synchronization settings at all, and to rely on Mac OS X's default behavior. With each release of Mac OS X, Apple has refined the default sync rules, and in Mac OS X 10.6 "Snow Leopard," the default rules are a very good starting point for many organizations. Some of the advantages of this approach are the following:

  - The end-user is free to customize the synchronization behavior using the Mobile Account Preferences dialog, available from the Accounts pane in System Preferences. Refer to Figure 12-2 for an example of this dialog.

  - Settings in the Mobile Account Preferences dialog are certain to match the effective settings; there's less likelihood of user confusion about expected synchronization behavior.

    And a big disadvantage is

■ There is no way to add exclusions to the sync rules. For example, if you'd rather not synchronize all of your users' iTunes music libraries, you have no way to exclude the `Music` folder other than politely asking your users to turn synchronization off for that folder.

■ *Set initial sync rules only (Manage "Once")*: This strategy relies on managing the synchronization preferences "Once." This is actually similar to the first strategy, with the added advantage that you get to customize the synchronization rules that the user starts with.

> You must be careful with the initial sync rules; it is possible to specify initial sync rules that cannot be properly displayed in the Mobile Account Preferences dialog.

A major disadvantage is that if you later discover you need to add additional exclusions, or add additional folders to the synchronization lists, this can be difficult to do without erasing any changes made by the user. (Recall that if you change a managed preference that is managed "Once," it is reapplied to all computers and/or users.) Later, we'll show an advanced technique to deal with this issue.

■ *Manage sync rules "Always"*: With this strategy, you take away the ability of the user to customize the synchronization rules. You take complete responsibility for managing the sync rules. In this case, you don't have to worry about the relationship between what is displayed in the Mobile Account Preferences dialog and the actual behavior, though it still might be confusing or frustrating to your users. When you manage the rules "Always," the controls in the Mobile Account Preferences dialog will appear disabled to indicate that they are not modifiable by the user.

■ *Manage some rules "Once" and some "Always"*: In theory, this could be the best strategy. You could add certain organization-specific changes to the exclusion lists, and even update them as needed, managing these "Always." The initial list of folders to synchronize could be managed "Once," allowing the users to modify the list if they would like.

However, in practice, not all combinations you can make with Workgroup Manager lead to configurations that provide good user feedback in the Mobile Account Preferences dialog. For example, let's say you added ~/Music to the Home Sync exclusion list, managed "Once," to turn off sync of the iTunes library. No indication of this setting would appear in the Mobile Account Preferences dialog. Your users might then assume their Music folder was being synchronized, and might be confused (or worse) when they discovered it was not. You'll need to very carefully select which preferences to manage "Always," which to manage "Once," and test their interaction with the Mobile Account Preferences dialog to make sure your managed settings don't lead to user confusion or frustration.

Table 12-1 shows how some of the combinations of managing some preferences "Once," and other preferences "Always" affect the availability of controls in the Mobile Account Preferences dialog.

Table 12-1. *How Mobility Rules Management Affects the Mobile Accounts Preferences Dialog*

	Workgroup Manager Mobility Rules			Mobile Account Preferences Behavior
	Preferences Sync	Home Sync	Options	
Manage:	Once	Once	Once	All controls enabled
Manage:	Always (Merge with user's settings selected)	Once	Once	Sync at login/logout checked, but inaccessible
Manage:	Always	Always	Once	Only sync frequency and menu bar status available
Manage:	Always	Always	Always	All controls disabled

Managing Synchronization Preferences Walkthrough

Let's do a step-by-step walkthrough of setting managed preferences for mobile account synchronization. We'll use the strategy of managing some rules "Once" and some "Always." This is the most complex of the suggested strategies—if you choose to implement one of the simpler strategies you should be able to follow this and make some simpler choices.

Using Workgroup Manager, start by creating a computer group named "HomeSync." Add one or more computers to this group for testing. Figure 12-7 shows an example.

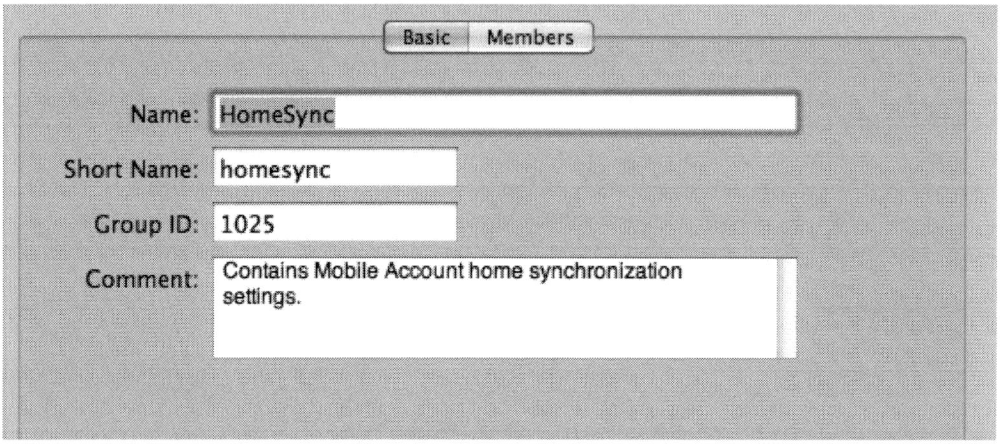

Figure 12-7. *HomeSync computer group in Workgroup Manager*

Switch to the Preferences Overview by clicking the Preferences icon in the toolbar. Click the Mobility icon to go to the editors for mobile account preferences. Select the "Rules" and "Preference Sync" tabs, as shown in Figure 12-8.

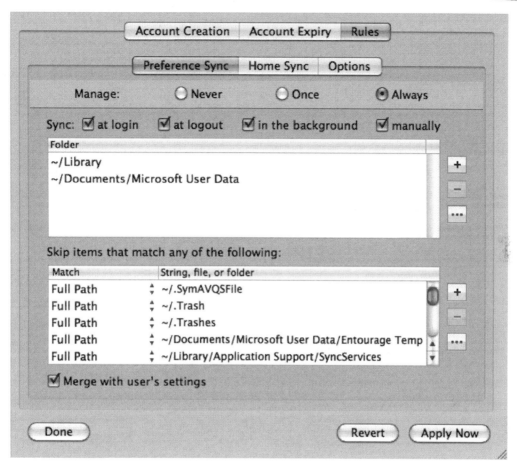

Figure 12-8. *Preference Sync settings*

Select "Manage: Always." Since there is no end-user interface for changing the settings for preference sync, if you manage this, you might as well manage it always. For this walkthrough, we'll leave everything here with its default value(s). If you have applications that create temporary files, caches, or indexes in ~/Library that should not be synchronized, you would add exclusions to the "Skip items that match any of the following" list. But for now, click "Apply Now" and select the "Home Sync" tab. The view should change to match Figure 12-9.

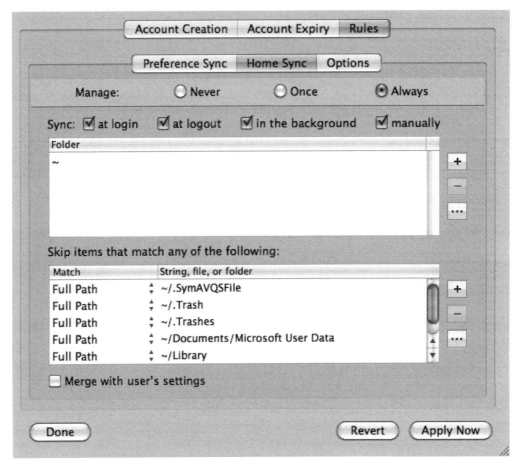

Figure 12-9. *Home Sync settings*

Again, set the management frequency to "Always" and leave everything else at its default value(s). Click "Apply Now" and then click the "Options" tab, which should change the view to match Figure 12-10.

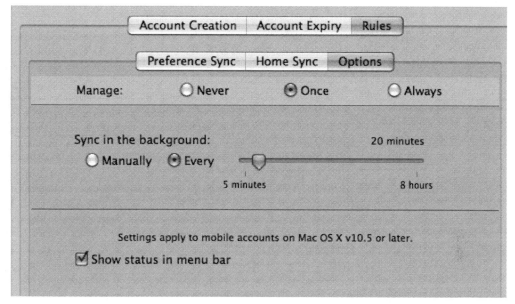

Figure 12-10. *Synchronization options*

For this group of preferences, we want the user to be able to change the synchronization frequency and remove the HomeSync menu from the menu bar if desired, so we'll manage this set of preferences "Once." Set the background sync time to 20 minutes, and check "Show status in menu bar." Click the "Apply Now" button.

Log in with a mobile account into a computer that is a member of the HomeSync computer group you just created. The Mobile Accounts Preferences dialog should look something like Figure 12-11.

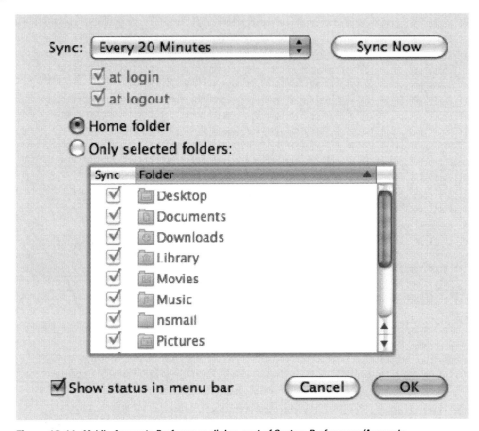

Figure 12-11. *Mobile Accounts Preferences dialog, part of System Preferences/Accounts*

The dialog does a fair job of reflecting the current managed settings. You can alter the periodic sync time, but cannot deselect login and logout sync, as these are managed "Always." The list of folders to synchronize looks like it could be changed, but if you click the "Only selected folders" radio button, you'll see that all of the subfolders are selected, but disabled.

What if we'd like the user to be able to modify more items in this dialog? For example, what if we'd like the user to be able to select only a few folders in his or her home for synchronization instead of the entire home? One solution would be to manage the Preference Sync items "Always," and manage the Home Sync items either "Never" or "Once." If we are using the default settings, "Once" gets us the same place as "Never," but if we need to customize the exclusion list, we'll want to use "Once." See Figure 12-12.

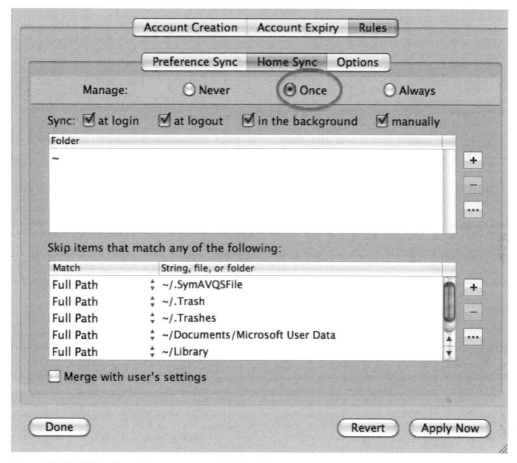

Figure 12-12. *Setting Home Sync management to "Once"*

Once we apply these changes and refresh preference management on our test machine (we can use `mcxrefresh`, or just restart), we should see that a user can now change which folders are synced as part of the Home Sync, as shown in Figure 12-13. Note that when "Only selected folders" is chosen, that "Library" is selected, but disabled. This is because the `Library` folder is part of the managed Preferences Sync, and so the user cannot modify synchronization for that folder.

Note also that the Mobile Account Preferences dialog does not display the exception list. This can lead to user confusion. If you were to add `~/Pictures` to the exclusion list, the contents of the user's `Pictures` folder would not be synced with the network home. Yet there would be no indication of this in the Mobile Account Preferences dialog. The user could choose to sync the home folder, or a set of specific folders including the `Pictures` folder, yet the invisible-to-the-end-user exclusion list would cause the `Pictures` folder to be excluded from synchronization. For this reason, you should be careful about adding items to the exclusion list that could cause confusion or possible data loss.

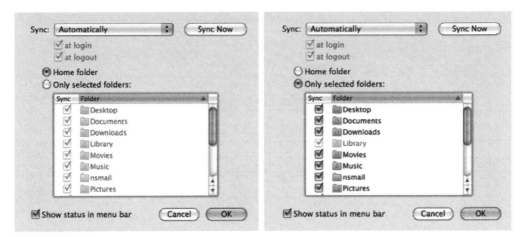

Figure 12-13. *User modification of Home Sync folders*

Limitations of Workgroup Manager's Preferences Overview

When using the Apple-provided preference editors, all of the settings on a single "page" are managed as a group. This is important to remember, especially when managing certain preferences "Once." Recall that if you make changes to a group of preferences managed "Once," they are applied once again.

Here is a specific example. In Figure 12-12, we managed the Home Sync settings "Once." We specified "~" as the sync folder, and we had a list of exclusions. If we apply these preferences "Once," the users are able to alter the list of folders to sync. Perhaps they decide they don't want to sync the entire home folder, and use the Mobile Accounts Preferences dialog (shown in Figure 12-13) to set synchronization only for their Desktop and Documents folders.

Later we determine that we need to add an item to the Home Sync exclusion list: we have an application that creates lock files for its documents, and the names of these lock files end with ".lockfile". If we add this exclusion to the exclusion list, as seen in Figure 12-14, and then apply these changes, the user who had set a list of synced folders to only the Desktop and Document folders will find the list reset to sync the entire home folder.

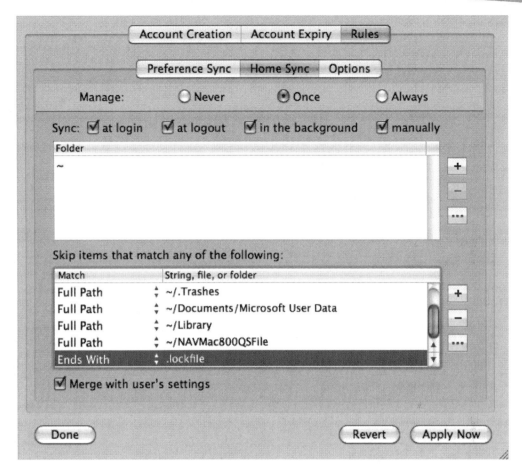

Figure 12-14. *Adding an item to the exclusion list*

The list of folders to sync is replaced because all of the preferences in Figure 12-14 are managed together as a set, and when you update one, they are all reapplied. This is probably not what we wanted. We probably intended for a change in the exclusion list to be applied by itself, leaving other settings alone. To get the flexibility we desire, we need to do a little more upfront planning and leave the comfortable world of the Preference Overview and its Apple-supplied preference editors.

What we want is to manage the list of synced folders and the exception list separately. We can do that by separating these settings into two computer groups.

Previously, we created a computer group named "HomeSync." Return to the Accounts editor in Workgroup Manager and create a new group called "HomeSyncExclusions." To this group add the same computer or computers that are members of the HomeSync computer group.

Switch to the Preferences Overview, and select the Mobility preferences. Select the "Rules" and "Home Sync" tabs, and manage these settings "Once." It should look the same as Figure 12-12, when we were editing the preferences in the "HomeSync" computer group. Click "Apply Now," and then the "Done" button.

Using the Preference Details Editor

Click the "Details" tab. It should now look something like Figure 12-15.

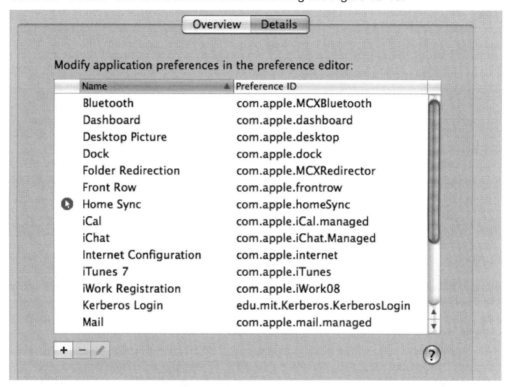

Figure 12-15. *Workgroup Manager Preferences Details pane*

NOTE: If the Preferences Details pane doesn't look anything like Figure 12-15, you probably haven't yet imported the preference manifests from Managed Client.app. For a review on importing a preference manifest, refer back to Chapter 10 (and please do so before continuing).

We're going to do some detail editing of the Home Sync preferences, so double-click the "Home Sync" entry. The details editor should look like the one shown in Figure 12-16.

NOTE: The gray circle with a white mouse pointer is an indication that there are some preferences already defined for that category. These were defined when we used the Preferences Overview Mobility editor.

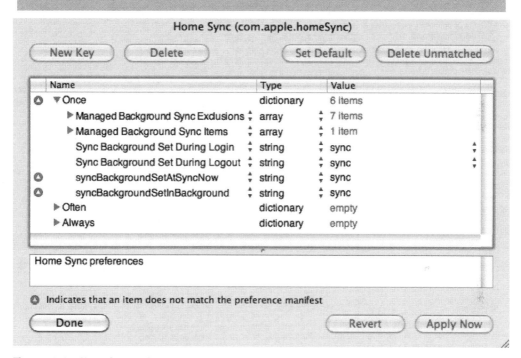

Figure 12-16. *Home Sync preferences detail*

We're interested in managing only the exclusion list, so delete everything except "Managed Background Sync Exclusions." The result appears in Figure 12-17.

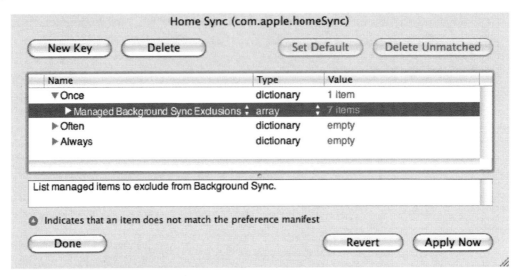

Figure 12-17. *Edited preferences list*

Click the "Apply Now" and "Done" buttons. To complete the division of the preferences, select the original "HomeSync" computer group, switch to the Preferences Details editor, and remove "Managed Background Sync Exclusions" from the "Once" section of the "Home Sync" preferences. The result should resemble Figure 12-18. The exact contents might vary; the important thing is to ensure the "Managed Background Sync Exclusions" are removed.

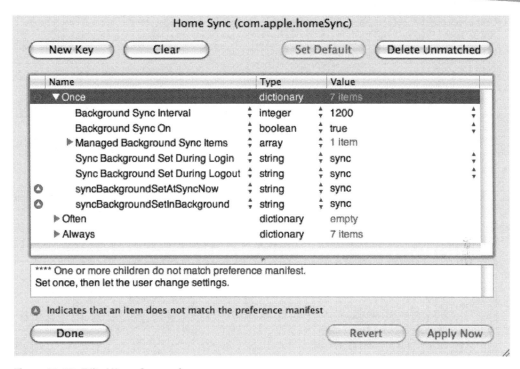

Figure 12-18. *Edited Home Sync preferences*

We now have two computer groups with managed preferences for Home Sync. One contains most of our Home Sync settings except for the exclusion list. The second group contains just the exclusion list. We can now update the exclusion list without worrying that it will reset other Home Sync choices made by our users.

This points out a general strategy when managing preferences "Once." The editors available via the Preferences Overview group sets of preferences together. If you think you may need to update a subset of these preferences without affecting user choices made for other items in this group of preferences, you should not use the editors in the Preferences Overview. Instead, you should use the Preferences Details editor and target the specific preferences you want to manage, instead of a larger group of related preferences.

> **NOTE:** You must also use the Preferences Details editor if you want to manage some items in a preference group "Once," and some "Always." With the editor in the Preference Overview, all the items in a particular group can be managed only one way: "Never," "Once," or "Always." Using the Preference Details editor gives you more precise control.

Once you've edited preferences with the Preference Details editor, there's no going back. If you try to edit the same preferences again with the Preferences Overview editors, you'll almost certainly undo your hard work.

Summary

Apple's Managed Preferences give you ways to manage mobile accounts that are difficult, if not impossible, to do any other way. You can use Managed Preferences to make it possible for end-users to create mobile accounts for themselves without the need for tech support assistance.

Other managed preferences can be utilized to enforce FileVault, cause mobile accounts to be created on removable media, and even limit the disk space used by the mobile home folder. Administrators can also automate the removal of old mobile accounts created on lab machines or other multi-user machines.

Managed preferences can be used to control the synchronization of the local home directory with the network home. You can control which folders are synchronized, how often the synchronization occurs, and specify exceptions to the synchronization.

Finally, we looked at ways to use advanced features of Workgroup Manager to provide more precise control over managed preferences to allow you to manage as much as possible while still allowing the end-user the ability to make changes. These strategies have uses outside of managing mobile accounts, and can be used for detailed management of other items.

Chapter **13**

Troubleshooting Managed Preferences

Whenever you start working with a new piece of software, be it a word processor, a video editor, a programming language, or a systems management framework, like Apple's Managed Preferences, you may run into problems.

Sometimes the problems you encounter will be of your own making—you misunderstand a feature, or you have not yet learned the proper way to accomplish a certain task. To fix these problems, you just need to do some more learning: re-read the documentation, find better documentation, ask for help on an Internet forum, or take a training class.

Sometimes the problems will be the fault of the software or its documentation—a feature doesn't really work as described, or wasn't properly implemented. You might be able to confirm the bug with the software vendor, or at least with other users of the same software. You then may need to figure out workarounds for these problems, or how to avoid the situations that trigger them.

Other problems fall somewhere in the middle: you may discover that the software wasn't really designed to do the thing you want it to do. Depending on your point of view, that might be a problem with your understanding, or a problem with the design of the software. In any case, you may find you'll have to turn to other tools to accomplish the thing you have in mind.

If you've read the book this far, we hope you now have a pretty good idea what Apple's Managed Preferences tools can do and what they can't. If you understand what Apple's Managed Client tools were designed for, you'll be able to avoid the problem of "wrong tool for the job." We also hope we've helped you develop a useful mental model of how Managed Preferences work. And as we've discussed various features and strategies, we've attempted to point out some potential pitfalls and problems you might encounter.

In this chapter, we'll show you where to look and what to look for when things aren't working as you'd expect.

Troubleshooting Triage

If you've managed or administered computer systems for a while, you may have developed some basic high-level troubleshooting techniques that help you quickly narrow down where to look for the source of a problem. Many of those same high-level techniques can help when troubleshooting Managed Preferences problems. So let's review a few now. Steps 1 and 2 are depicted in Figures 13-1 and 13-2, followed by step 3.

Triage Step 1: Did It Ever Work?

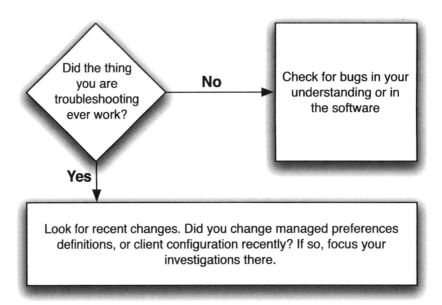

Figure 13-1. *Triage step 1: Did it ever work?*

Triage Step 2: Machine- or User-Specific?

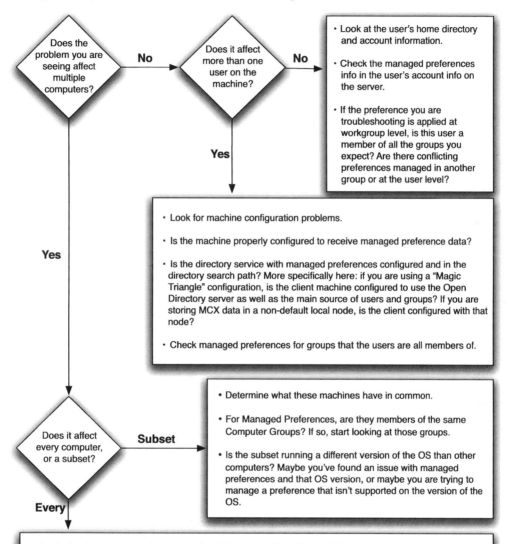

Figure 13-2. *Triage step 2: Machine- or user-specific?*

Triage Step 3: Simplify

Another important technique when triaging a problem is to simplify:

■ Try to eliminate all other factors and reproduce the problem in as simple a manner as possible. Applied to managed preferences, this could mean creating a new user or computer object and managing a single preference. If you can verify that it works as expected, you can systematically add additional managed preferences into the mix until it breaks. This can help you discover a preferences interaction that is the cause of your undesired results.

■ On the other hand, if it still doesn't work when boiled down to its simplest elements, you've probably encountered a bug, either in the software or in your understanding of the software.

You might be surprised how often stressed systems administrators skip the high-level triage steps and get lost in the details, sifting through logs and checking anything and everything they can think of, without taking a breath, stepping back, and doing some steps to narrow down the places to look.

Examining Delivered Managed Preferences

Let's assume you've done your troubleshooting triage and have narrowed down your areas of investigation. You believe it to be a problem with a certain managed preference.

Most managed preferences problems fall into one of two categories:

1. The managed preference is not being delivered to the machine/user.

2. The managed preference is not behaving as you expect.

To determine which type of problem you have, the first thing you'll want to do is examine what managed preferences, if any, are currently in effect on the computer with the problem you are troubleshooting. If you can confirm the managed preference you are troubleshooting is actually in effect, you probably have the second kind of problem. Otherwise, your problem falls into the first category. You have two main tools for examining which preferences have been delivered to your computers: mcxquery and System Profiler, both of which were introduced and discussed in Chapter 8. Refer back to that chapter for a quick refresher, if needed. Let's look at them again right now in the context of the two problems.

mcxquery

The first tool is run from the command line on the troublesome computer: mcxquery. If you call it without any additional options, it will return all the managed preferences data in effect for the current user, current workgroup, and current computer—in other words, all the managed preferences currently in effect.

```
> mcxquery
com.apple.virtualMemory
    UseEncryptedSwap                            securevm     often   1
                                                (Computer
                                                Group)

com.microsoft.autoupdate2
    HowToCheck                                  office2008   often   Manual
                                                (Computer
                                                Group)
com.microsoft.Excel
    2008\Default Save\Default Format            office2008   once    57
                                                (Computer
                                                Group)
com.microsoft.office
    2008\FirstRun\SetupAssistCompleted          office2008   often   1
                                                (Computer
                                                Group)
com.microsoft.Powerpoint
    2008\Default Save\Default Save\Default Format  office2008 once   Microsoft
                                                (Computer            PowerPoint 98
                                                Group)              Presentation
com.microsoft.Word
    2008\Default Save\Default Format            office2008   once    Doc97
                                                (Computer
                                                Group)
```

Here we can easily see (among other things) the Office 2008–related managed preferences that are in effect for the current user of this machine. So we know at least that some managed preferences are being delivered.

For each managed preference, you are given information on what directory service record the data is coming from, the management frequency, and the value of the preference. In this example, the Office 2008 managed preferences are coming from the "office2008" computer group. If we expected to see Office 2008 preferences, but did not, we'd then want to check to make sure the current computer was a member of the "office2008" computer group.

If the current user did not have the Office 2008 preferences we expected, the output of mcxquery might show us a managed preference interaction we weren't aware of or had forgotten.

NOTE: We covered managed preference interactions in Chapter 8, "Compositing Preferences."

Managed Preference Interaction Example

Here's an example of a managed preference interaction. Let's say user John Doe kept having the Microsoft AutoUpdate application notify him of available Office updates. As a non-admin user, he has no way to install these, so he finds the notifications just annoying. (And he's starting to wonder why you, the systems administrator, haven't already taken care of these updates!) Worse, even though every time it comes up he sets it to check only manually, it keeps getting reset to check automatically. As the administrator, you thought you had managed preferences for all your machines to disable automatic checking for Office updates, and indeed, no one else is reporting this issue. So to begin troubleshooting, let's check the managed preferences for John.

```
> sudo mcxquery -user jdoe
com.microsoft.autoupdate2
     HowToCheck                                         jdoe      often   Automatic
                                                        (User)
     WhenToCheck                                        jdoe      often   1
                                                        (User)
com.microsoft.Excel
     2008\Default Save\Default Format                   office2008 once   57
                                                        (Computer
                                                        Group)
com.microsoft.office
     2008\FirstRun\SetupAssistCompleted                 office2008 often  1
                                                        (Computer
                                                        Group)
com.microsoft.Powerpoint
     2008\Default Save\Default Save\Default Format       office2008 once   Microsoft
                                                        (Computer        PowerPoint 98
                                                        Group)           Presentation
com.microsoft.Word
     2008\Default Save\Default Format                   office2008 once   Doc97
                                                        (Computer
                                                        Group)
```

We quickly see that there is managed preferences data in John Doe's user record in the directory, and the com.microsoft.autoupdate2 settings in his user record take precedence over those in the office2008 computer group. With this new information, we can now delete the managed preferences for com.microsoft.autoupdate2 in John Doe's user record to allow the preferences we want to take effect. We can use Workgroup Manager or dscl to make these changes; most likely you'll use the same tool you use to create and edit all of your managed preferences data.

System Profiler

The other tool you can use to examine managed preferences data on a client machine is Apple's System Profiler application. You'll find this application in the /Applications/ Utilities folder on your startup disk. One of the many pieces of data it can retrieve for you is Managed Client information, which is an Apple term for what we've been calling managed preferences. (You may remember that "MCX" apparently stands for "Managed

Client for OS X".) Figure 13-3 shows some of the same Office 2008 managed preferences data we were looking at with `mcxquery`.

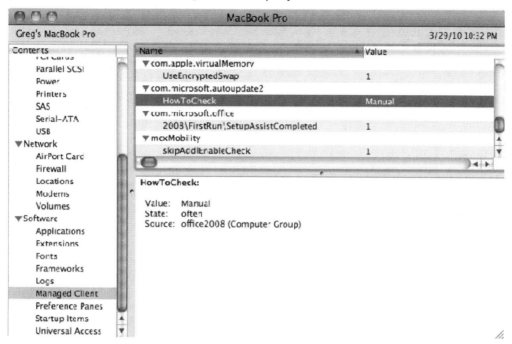

Figure 13-3. *System Profiler displaying managed preferences data*

If you're paying close attention, you'll notice that the "com.microsoft" managed preferences displayed in System Profiler are a subset of those returned by `mcxquery`. Further investigation shows that only items managed "often" or "always" are shown here. Items managed "once" might appear, but only during the login session during which they were initially applied.

> **NOTE:** We covered preference management frequencies—"Never," "Once," "Often," and "Always"—in Chapter 9.

Though perhaps easier to use than `mcxquery`, System Profiler gives less complete data. Still, it can be a quick and convenient way to confirm that managed preferences are at least being delivered to the machine. You should not rely on the data from System Profiler as definitive; use `mcxquery` for a more accurate view of managed preferences.

> **NOTE:** System Profiler (and its command-line equivalent, system_profiler) has an additional limitation. System Profiler actually displays only the preferences cached in /Library/Managed Preferences. If you have deleted these while troubleshooting, System Profiler may display "No information available" when asked to show Managed Client data. Generally, a restart will repopulate the contents of /Library/Managed Preferences. mcxquery does not rely on this cached data; instead it gets its information from the directory service.

MCX Caching

In Mac OS X 10.4 Tiger, some frequently seen problems with managed preferences were caused by MCX caching. Tiger cached MCX preferences locally for performance reasons. Occasionally, changes to managed preferences on the directory server were not immediately applied to local machines because the local machine was still using cached settings. Administrators could clear the local MCX cache with a special command:

```
sudo /System/Library/CoreServices/mcxd.app/Contents/Resources/MCXCacher -f
```

This command flushes the local cache, forcing the machine to re-read its managed preferences data from the network directory service, and causing the cached data to match the data available from the directory service.

The MCXCacher command was removed in Mac OS X 10.5 Leopard. In Leopard and Snow Leopard, MCX is cached only for offline use, and not for performance. According to Apple, when the managed preferences directory service is available, the MCX cache is not used. Therefore, clearing the cache should almost never be needed. But theory rarely matches practice. If, as part of troubleshooting, you want to remove any locally cached MCX data, you can do the following (where <localcomputerrecord> corresponds to the local computer record):

```
sudo dscl . -delete /Computers/<localcomputerrecord>
```

This does not clear cached MCX data for mobile accounts. If you have any users with mobile accounts on the machine you are troubleshooting, you can clear the cached MCX data for those accounts by deleting the "MCXSettings," "MCXFlags," and "cached_groups" attributes from the mobile account record. You can use dscl for this task, but be careful.

> **CAUTION:** Do not use `dscl` to delete the /Computers/<localcomputerrecord> from the local directory service if you are storing your managed preferences data in the default local directory node, as described in Chapter 7. In this configuration, the data in the local directory's `/Computers` objects is not a cache, but the actual data itself!
>
> In Snow Leopard, there is a "localhost" computer record in the local directory service. Don't delete that record.
>
> Likewise, be extra careful when using `dscl` to delete MCX attributes from mobile accounts. A typo could easily delete the entire user record.

Troubleshooting Local MCX

Since storing managed preferences data in the local directory service is a special configuration, there are a few special troubleshooting techniques that do not apply to more traditional network directory configurations. We discuss them here.

No Managed Preferences Data

One of the more common issues you might see with Local MCX, especially when you are first setting it up, is that no managed preferences data is being applied. You can see this with `mcxquery` or System Profiler—neither will show managed preferences data. Here are some things to check.

Directory Service Search Path

If you are using a non-default local node, like `/Local/MCX` instead of `/Local/Default`, did you remember to add the node to the Directory Service authentication search path? See Chapter 6 if you don't recall how to do this.

You can use Directory Utility, or the `dscl` command to check:

```
dscl /Search read / SearchPath
```

(The space between the forward slash and "SearchPath" is important.)

Local Computer Record

If you are managing preferences at the computer or computer group level, is there a local computer record with the current machine's Ethernet ID?

Here's how to find a computer record for the current machine. First, get the Ethernet ID for the machine:

```
> ifconfig en0 | awk '/ether/ {print $2}'
00:26:4a:0a:61:62
```

Next, use dscl to search for a computer record with that value for the ENetAddress:

```
> dscl /Search search /Computers ENetAddress 00:26:4a:0a:61:62
local_laptop              ENetAddress = (
    "00:26:4a:0a:61:62"
)
local_laptop              ENetAddress = (
    "00:26:4a:0a:61:62"
)
```

There appear to be two computer records with this machine's Ethernet ID, both named "local_laptop". Let's find out which directories they are in:

```
> dscl /Search read /Computers/local_laptop dsAttrTypeStandard:AppleMetaNodeLocation
AppleMetaNodeLocation: /Local/Default
AppleMetaNodeLocation: /Local/MCX
```

One record is in /Local/Default, and the other is in the /Local/MCX node (I'm using an alternate local node, as described in Chapter 7, under "Advanced Local MCX"). Since the MCX framework caches computer data in a computer record in the /Local/Default node, this is expected. In fact, if our applicable computer record was on a network directory service, we'd still have a local cached copy in the local directory service in /Local/Default.

NOTE: The fact that the currently active computer record is cached in the default local node (unless you are storing MCX data for computers and computer groups there) suggests another way to check the computer record.

First, list the computer records in the default local node:

```
> dscl . list /Computers
local_desktop
localhost
```

In Snow Leopard, the operating system creates a localhost record, so we can ignore that for now. So our cached local computer object must be called "local_desktop". We can use `dscl` to find out where it was cached from:

```
> dscl . read /Computers/local_desktop
dsAttrTypeStandard:OriginalNodeName
OriginalNodeName: /Local/MCX
```

So the original "local_desktop" record is in the `/Local/MCX` directory node, and is being cached in `/Local/Default`. If your managed preferences data is coming from a network directory service, you'd see the name of that service:

```
OriginalNodeName: /LDAPv3/od.pretendco.com
OriginalNodeName: /Active Directory/ad.pretendco.com
```

Of course, as the systems administrator, you probably won't have to go through all these gyrations to find the local computer record, since presumably you are the one who created it! Just look in the same place you created it and verify it has the right Ethernet ID, as in Figure 13-4.

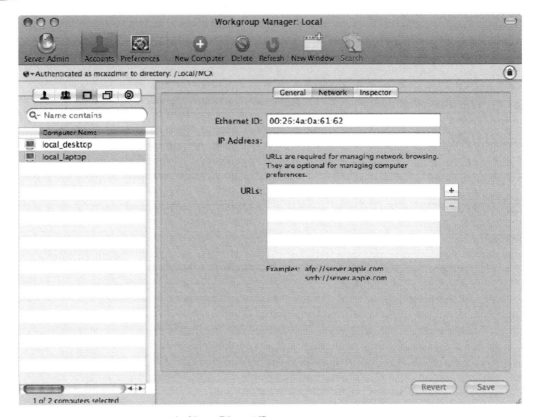

Figure 13-4. *Local computer record with our Ethernet ID*

If you can't find a functional computer record for the current machine, you'd better create one, or add the correct Ethernet ID to one. With any luck, as in Chapter 7, you have a script for just that purpose.

Wrong or Old Managed Preferences Data

Another commonly encountered issue is wrong or old managed preferences data on a particular machine. Remember that in this configuration you are storing managed preferences data in a node of the local directory service. In other words, the data is just .plist files in directories under /private/var/db/dslocal/nodes/. So the most common reason for wrong or old MCX data is that updated versions of these .plist files have not been pushed out to the current machine via whatever file/software delivery mechanism you have: Puppet, Radmind, ARD, a package-based installer, or whatever. Or, equally likely, you have old data here that used to be managed, but that has been forgotten or abandoned.

To fix this issue, make sure your file/software delivery mechanism is running and has delivered the latest versions of the appropriate `.plist` files. If your file/software delivery mechanism doesn't clean up old data, you may need to do it manually.

This actually brings up another point: if you are using a file or software delivery mechanism to update your Local MCX data, Directory Service may not see your changes right away, and the managed preferences in effect will not update right away, either.

To make Directory Service re-read the `.plist` files and pick up any changes, issue this command:

```
> sudo killall DirectoryService
```

This causes Directory Service to quit and relaunch. Upon relaunching, Directory Service will re-read all the `.plist` files in the local directory nodes.

> **NOTE:** Our technical reviewer assures us that "killall –HUP DirectoryService" works as well in most cases, and avoids terminating the Directory Service process.

Even after forcing Directory Service to re-read all its local data, managed preferences settings that you have changed may not be applied until the current user logs out and back in.

> **NOTE:** This behavior is not unique to Local MCX. Most managed preferences changes don't take effect until the next login, or until `mcxrefresh` is executed.

mcxrefresh

This brings us to a new tool introduced in Mac OS X 10.6 Snow Leopard, `mcxrefresh`. As we've mentioned, under normal circumstances, new or updated managed preferences don't usually take effect immediately. In many cases, changed managed preferences are not applied until the next login. If you are testing some changes to managed preferences, it can be tedious and time-consuming to log out and back in after each change you make. You can use `mcxrefresh` to force a client to re-read its managed preferences from the server (or directory service) without needing to log out and back in.

The syntax is simple:

```
sudo mcxrefresh -n usershortname
sudo mcxrefresh -u <uid>
```

mcxrefresh must be run as root or via sudo. If your managed preferences data is coming from an Active Directory server, add the –a flag, which will ask for authentication to pass to Active Directory:

```
sudo mcxrefresh -n shortusername -a
```

If there are no errors, mcxrefresh just silently returns without printing anything to the Terminal.

Most mcxrefresh error messages are pretty easy to understand:

```
> sudo mcxrefresh -n freddykrueger
2010-03-31 16:50:43.303 mcxrefresh[322:903] mcxrefresh: unable to locate 'freddykrueger'
2010-03-31 16:50:43.307 mcxrefresh[322:903] mcxrefresh- returned error status 3
```

(There is no user named "freddykrueger" in the available directories.)

```
> sudo mcxrefresh
2010-03-31 16:51:16.706 mcxrefresh[351:903] mcxrefresh- requires uid or username
parameter
2010-03-31 16:51:16.709 mcxrefresh[351:903] mcxrefresh- returned error status 1
```

(You forgot to pass a username or uid.)

There is one error that's a little less obvious:

```
> sudo mcxrefresh -n gneagle
Wed Mar 31 16:50:55 macbookpro.pretendco.com ManagedClient[324] <Error>:
kCGErrorFailure: Set a breakpoint @ CGErrorBreakpoint() to catch errors as they are
logged.
```

This actually isn't an error from mcxrefresh; it's coming from ManagedClient, yet another Mac OS X process that deals with managed preferences. Some clues about what triggers this error are the names kCGErrorFailure and CGErrorBreakpoint(). The "CG" in each of these names refers to CoreGraphics, one of the subsystems of OS X. A little experimentation shows us that this error is generated if you run mcxrefresh and give it the name or uid of a user who isn't currently logged in at a GUI session. If I log in at the login window as "gneagle" and run the command again, it returns quietly:

```
> sudo mcxrefresh -n gneagle
>
```

A quiet return like this is a good sign. Managed preferences data has been successfully refreshed for user gneagle.

One More Thing...

If using mcxrefresh doesn't work, or you're working with a Mac OS X 10.5 machine (which doesn't have mcxrefresh), there is one more option. In Chapter 8, we talked about MCXCompositor. MCXCompositor composites or brings together an aggregate of all preferences from all sources that are applied to the machine or users of that machine. It then stores the result in /Library/Managed Preferences. We've seen cases where this cache of data is a bit more tenacious than it should be. Since this is ultimately where Mac OS X is deriving its preference information from (for the specific cases that the Managed Preferences override), if /Library/Managed Preferences has old or incorrect data, you'll see behavior other than you'd expect.

You may find that you've updated Managed Preferences at the source—in other words, in a directory—but a user is saying that the previous behavior still exists, even after a logout and login. In this case, don't be afraid to wipe the contents of /Library/Managed Preferences and then reboot. The contents of this directory will be regenerated by MCXCompositor.

> **NOTE:** Be sure to run mcxrefresh (if available) or reboot after clearing the contents of /Library/Managed Preferences. If you don't, managed preferences will not be in effect.

If this is happening often, you can use mcxquery to see if the changes you expect are reflected in the cache at /Library/Managed Preferences. Often, though, it's not worth the trouble, as this tends to be a rare condition. If this does happen more than once to users of a particular machine, deeper investigation is warranted into other subsystems (e.g., have you run a disk check lately?).

Summary

In this chapter, we looked at some troubleshooting strategies and tools to use when investigating the cause of a managed preferences problem. We described some high-level troubleshooting steps one can do to narrow down the number of places to look. We demonstrated the use of both mcxquery and the System Profiler application to determine which managed preferences are being applied to a given client machine.

Next, we looked at the special problem of troubleshooting managed preferences data stored in the local directory store (Local MCX) and gave tips on troubleshooting that somewhat unique configuration.

Finally, we wrapped up with a quick examination of the mcxrefresh tool, which can help troubleshoot a problem faster by allowing you to test newly changed managed preferences on a client machine without taking the time to log out/in or reboot.

Index

You Need the Companion eBook

Your purchase of this book entitles you to buy the companion PDF-version eBook for only $10. Take the weightless companion with you anywhere.

We believe this Apress title will prove so indispensable that you'll want to carry it with you everywhere, which is why we are offering the companion eBook (in PDF format) for $10 to customers who purchase this book now. Convenient and fully searchable, the PDF version of any content-rich, page-heavy Apress book makes a valuable addition to your programming library. You can easily find and copy code—or perform examples by quickly toggling between instructions and the application. Even simultaneously tackling a donut, diet soda, and complex code becomes simplified with hands-free eBooks!

Once you purchase your book, getting the $10 companion eBook is simple:

❶ Visit **www.apress.com/promo/tendollars/**.

❷ Complete a basic registration form to receive a randomly generated question about this title.

❸ Answer the question correctly in 60 seconds, and you will receive a promotional code to redeem for the $10.00 eBook.

THE EXPERT'S VOICE™

233 Spring Street, New York, NY 10013

Offer valid through 11/10.

Made in the USA
Lexington, KY
03 February 2016